The Work of the Harbour Master

third edition

by

The Nautical Institute

in association with the

the International Harbour Masters' Association

The Work of the Harbour Master

third edition

by

The Nautical Institute

in association with the

the International Harbour Masters' Association

Published by The Nautical Institute

202 Lambeth Road, London SE1 7LQ, UK

Tel: +44 (0)20 7928 1351 Fax: +44 (0)20 7401 2817 Web: www.nautinst.org

Book Editor Andrew Lansdale
Design and typesetting by PMD Visual Communications
Printed in the UK by Geerings Print Ltd

ISBN 978 1 906915 02 5

Foreword

by **Capt James Robinson** DSM FNI Irish Navy (Retired)
President
The Nautical Institute

The work of the Harbour Master is not widely understood; indeed it could be said that it is often misunderstood. This is hardly surprising as it can vary so widely from country to country and even from port to port within countries. In addition, the role of the Harbour Master continues to evolve with modern Harbour Masters finding themselves working in new areas and shouldering responsibilities outside what might have been regarded as the traditional role.

Responsibilities vary between ports; therefore this book cannot explain everything Harbour Masters everywhere may be expected to undertake as part of their jobs. However, it can show, from the experience of others some examples of what they may encounter.

Traditionally Harbour Masters have been ex-seafarers, however, increasingly non mariners will be taking up some of these posts. This is an inevitable result of the shortage of candidates who have sufficient sea-time to gain the experience and qualifications necessary to come ashore to take up such important posts. Even experienced mariners will find that the learning curve is steep as they take the step from Shipmaster to Harbour Master.

Anyone assuming the Harbour Master role, whatever their background, will need support. This book will help to provide that. In addition The Nautical Institute has devised a qualification which is recognised worldwide and offers aspirants the opportunity to complete the Harbour Master Certificate Scheme. This book will be a support to that scheme, which is regularly reviewed and updated. The importance of the Scheme will only grow in the future as more non mariners become Harbour Masters.

In all these cases The Nautical Institute and the International Harbour Masters' Association have worked together to try to find some answers or some explanations. The aim of the volume is to provide a bridge to the Harbour Master role for anyone new to it or new to aspects of the job.

Its strength lies in the collaboration between the Institute and the IHMA which has brought together authors who have contributed their experiences to the book and peer reviewers to scrutinise each chapter to ensure as many aspects of HM activities as possible are covered.

The work of members of both organisations shows the worth of professional membership bodies. Their members work to improve knowledge and implement best practice. Through the exchange of ideas, of which this book is a sophisticated version, they offer help to those new to the industry and those progressing through to more senior positions or undertaking continuing professional development (CPD). In the case of the Institute, we can help promote best practice and the exchange of experiences through our publications, our worldwide branch structure and our conferences, including our prestigious Command Seminar series.

Many people have freely given of their time and expertise in this book. Both the Institute and the IHMA are grateful to them. The book is the richer for it. The Harbour Master role is increasingly complex against the background of developing world trade. All practitioners must be professional. Both our organisations can support that.

Acknowledgements

Many individuals and organisations have contributed to the writing of this book and its peer review. Special thanks are due to the following for their advice on chapter content and peer review: Captain Mark Andrews MNI, Milford Haven Port Authority, UK; Captain Eric Atkinson FNI, Fremantle Ports Authority, Australia; Vasily Belyaev, Port of Kaliningrad, Russia; Don Cockrill, International Maritime Pilots Association; Alan Coghlan, President, IMHA; Captain Lindsay Copeman MNI, Port Hedland Port Authority, Australia; John Dickinson FNI, The Nautical Institute; Martin Donnelly MNI, Drogheda Port Company, Ireland; Mike Hadley FNI, IHMA; Captain Rufus Lekala, Port of Durban, South Africa; Jaap Lems, Port of Rotterdam Authority, Netherlands; Alan Loynd FNI, Branscombe Marine Consultants, Hong Kong; Captain Andreas Mai, Chairman, European Harbour Masters' Committee and Bremen and Bremerhaven, Germany; Captain Saleem Al-Mabsly, Port Sultan Qaboos-Muscat, Oman; Kevin Richardson, Port of Dover, UK; Ingrid Römers, Port of Rotterdam Authority, Netherlands and Secretary, European Harbour Masters' Committee; Captain Ben van Scherpenzeel, Senior Technical Adviser, Port of Rotterdam Authority, Netherlands; Alexander Surikov, Port of Primorsk Authority, Russia; Dirk Vernaeve, Port of Ghent, Belgium, Chairman of the IHMA Papers Committee; Mike Wier FNI, Whitstable Harbour, UK.

Contents

Introduction .... **vii**
by Alan Coghlan

Chapter 1: Harbour Master – a profession defined **1**
by Ingrid Römers

Chapter 2: The Harbour Master and the port approach area **9**
by Alan Coghlan

Chapter 3: Maritime port and terminal information **16**
by Captain Ing Ben van Scherpenzeel

Chapter 4: The Harbour Master and vessel traffic services **27**
by Jillian Carson-Jackson M Ed MNI AFRIN

Chapter 5: The Harbour Master and pilot relationships **35**
by John Dickinson FNI

Chapter 6 The Harbour Master and tug operations **40**
by John Lee-Richards

Chapter 7: The Harbour Master and the mooring process **47**
by Captain Ing. Ben van Scherpenzeel

Chapter 8: The Harbour Master and terminal and cargo operations **56**
by Alan Coghlan

Chapter 9: The Harbour Master and port security **63**
Landside security by Alexander Surikov
Waterside security by Jaap Lems

Chapter 10: The Harbour Master and the environment **70**
by Geraldine Knatz

Chapter 11: The Harbour Master and port safety **80**
by Alan Coghlan

Chapter 12: The Harbour Master and incidents 89
by Mark Andrews

Chapter 13: The Harbour Master and the local community 97
by Captain Sean Bolt BA M.Prof Stud FCILT

Chapter 14: The Harbour Master and the media 103
by James Herbert

Chapter 15: The Harbour Master and rules and regulations – case study, Mediterranean 111
by Captain Reuben Lanfranco LLM MCIT AFM FNI

Chapter 16: The Harbour Master and management, finances, training and education 117
by Kevin Richardson

Chapter 17: The Harbour Master and professional membership 130
by Ingrid Römers and Bridget Hogan

image: Portpictures

Introduction

By **Alan Coghlan**
President, the International Harbour Masters' Association

What's in a name? When it comes to Harbour Masters this is not a rhetorical question. It was and still is an interesting issue when uniting Harbour Masters worldwide in one association. This is quite a challenge because of the many differences in job descriptions that cover the Harbour Master role.

There are ports where no person has the title of Harbour Master; even so, in these ports someone will execute the broad set of duties that in general are assigned to that role. The suggestion is regularly made to rename the title of Harbour Master as a description of the job. But then again, the term is too well known and too much cherished. And it is understood in all maritime circles. So we will continue with that title.

Hence this third edition of *The Work of the Harbour Master* seeks to help all those who have taken on aspects of this complex and unique role in ports – whatever your job title may be. The book describes many aspects of the job and it will appeal those who provide safe ports, who organise safe passage for vessels and who are in charge of port marine operations. All will gain something from some sections, if not all of them. The chapter sequence takes you through the passage of a ship as it enters the port to the berth and explains the role of the Harbour Master through the sections of this voyage.

The book is a practical one and many experienced Harbour Masters share their experiences. It gives a realistic impression of what may be faced by prospective Harbour Masters, or those who find their duties or responsibilities changing. Many people from IHMA and The Nautical Institute have been involved with this book. Their breadth of experience and geographical spread illustrates clearly the universal nature of the Harbour Master post.

image: Portpictures

Chapter 1

Harbour Master – a profession defined

By **Ingrid Römers** – Secretary European Harbour Masters' Committee
Senior Advisor Harbour Master Division Port of Rotterdam

In every discussion that concerns Harbour Masters, their duties and the way they exercise them, there is always someone in the group who says: "I see where you're coming from, but we are all different". And it is true, all Harbour Masters are different, their ports are different, by ownership, geographically, in complexity and in types of trade. In all the ways they can be, they are different.

Even the name that Harbour Masters go by is different around the world. Probably Harbour Master is the one most understood, but others with titles such as port captain, chief port officer or marine operations manager may have a role in port safety and environment and the management of port marine operations. This role may be one of great responsibility. On the other hand, the role of a 'genuine' Harbour Master may be one with a small part of the port's operational area to oversee. Hence requests to define the Harbour Master role more precisely arise regularly. When deciding what makes up a Harbour Master profile, one first encounters a lot of differences in factors that individuals cannot influence.

Every port is different in the trade it handles: oil, chemicals, containers, coal and other dry bulk, ferry traffic, fishing, export-orientated ports, import-orientated ports, short sea ports, deep sea hubs and combinations of all of these. All ports deal with vessels with specific characteristics and different cargo operation requirements.

Geography also offers a wide ranging disparity. One port may be easily accessible, another one difficult to access. The complexity of a port is not a matter of size. A small port may be a highly complex one and pose some navigational challenges to vessels. This may be the case when its location is more inland, or if the waters are shallow rather than deep. There are also currents and large tidal differences to add to a port's complexity. The risk assessment that goes with such characteristics determines the risk control option Harbour Masters may want to put in place.

Another influence on the role of Harbour Masters will be the organisation that has responsibility for their ports. Some ports are governed by Acts of Parliament or by regional or local governments. Others are privately-owned while some aspects of operation may be in the hands of central or local government. A number of port authorities have evolved over the years into more autonomous structures, either public or private, in order to be more competitive and market-oriented. These different ownership and governance structures have an effect on the level of autonomy of Harbour Masters.

The European Sea Ports Organisation (ESPO) investigated the role Harbour Masters in Europe play in port authorities' organisational structures. Most respondents – 57.3% – said Harbour Masters constitute a part of the port authority. Certainly this seems to be the case in northern Europe. In southern Europe it is a different story. Here, where Harbour Masters head the marine department, they may work with an independent public entity such as the Coast Guard, or be under the direct control of a national or local ministry such as transport, but sometimes also defence, or sometimes a maritime administration.

Another element which highlights the different paths Harbour Masters find themselves taking is the lack of a worldwide or even regionally agreed required qualifications for them.

These differences combine to ensure the responsibilities and tasks Harbour Masters undertake vary between ports. Some may actually be political appointees with working Harbour Masters working under them. They, in turn, will have specialists working for them. At the other end of the spectrum, Harbour Masters, especially in smaller ports, will be expected to do everything.

This is a very complex picture and presents the Harbour Master with a big task to take everything into account and produce a safe, working port. However, we can make some generalisations of the types of activity that Harbour Masters are engaged in, wherever they are.

Harbour Masters' main activities are in the approach area, the fairways leading to and from the port harbour basins and movement within them. These activities are aimed at ensuring safe, smooth, environmentally friendly water- and ship-related activities, during transit and during mooring or anchoring in the port. Harbour Masters need to ensure all the complex processes work to this aim.

Issues faced by ports today also include the environment, planning, dealing with those who live near to the port and cultural aspects, if indigenous people are involved. The demands of big ships and small boats will need to be reconciled where ports combine trade and recreational activities. Sometimes there is the challenge of a one-off event such as the Olympics or the Volvo Ocean Race. Often these projects will fall to the Harbour Master.

So this here is an attempt to define the Harbour Master role even for those who work under another title.

The role is likely to break down into two distinct areas: the statutory role and the ship-shore interface role. It is these two distinct instruments that Harbour Masters may have at their disposal; the formal powers and the operational assignment. These two aspects, the regulatory role and exercise of jurisdiction and, on the other hand, the wider role as the ship-shore interface, form the building blocks of the profession. The tasks and duties that go with these building blocks cover the whole spectrum of mastering a port. Harbour Masters may be active in all of them, or they may be assigned for some, or just one of them. They are no less Harbour Masters but have a different emphasis to their roles and functions.

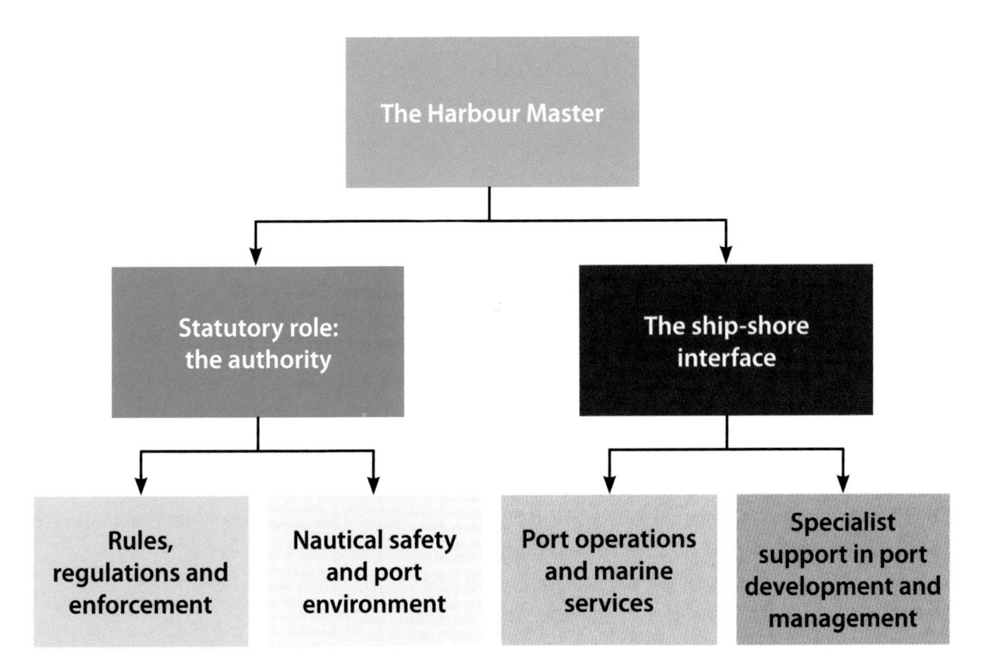

1.1 The Harbour Master defined

The authority

Running a safe port necessitates an independent authority and this will in many cases be the Harbour Master. If the Harbour Master role includes this statutory role, then they will be given powers to draft and enforce port byelaws and legislation covering maritime operations, safety and the environment. Other duties will include drafting admission policies.

This statutory role is not to be confused with the port authority; the organisation that governs the port. This governing body is generally responsible for the development of the port, the lease of land, port finances, spatial planning, intermodal networks, promotion activities and so on. Harbour Masters may be charged with their statutory task as part of the port authority. They may also have their own, sometimes quite autonomous, responsibilities.

The ship-shore interface

The second role concerns the marine operations in the port. Not only are they to be done in a safe and environmentally friendly manner, but smoothly as well: this forms the ship-shore interface. This involves dealing with the running of a port and port operations other then from a regulatory position. As the ship-shore interface, the Harbour Master is the person ashore who forms a bridge to the ship. They have a role in planning marine port operations, in the operation of bridges and locks and in the nautical technical services for ships; pilotage, mooring and tug operations.

Finally, Harbour Masters may sit on the management boards of the port authorities or otherwise make a contribution to management of their ports by offering specialist advice.

1.2 The Harbour Master's duties and tasks

The authority: rules, regulations and enforcement

Nautical safety and care for the environment is governed by numerous laws and regulations. Harbour Masters have to not only obey them but also enforce them. They may also be authorised to draft byelaws for their own ports. These port byelaws and admission policies set the conditions under which vessels may enter and leave the port and berth at or in specific areas within the port.

Ships that carry dangerous goods are bound by stricter regulations. Here the Harbour Master is also governed by international legislation. There are ports, notably those ports that tranship quantities of oil, oil products and chemicals, in which more than half of all transhipments are classified as hazardous and noxious cargoes.

The IMO's International Maritime Dangerous Goods Code (IMDG) regulates the transportation of dangerous and noxious goods, and their handling in ports. Harbour Masters may have a supervisory or enforcement role in the IMDG code or parts of the Code. In view of this, a large part of their own port byelaws will be concerned with the transport and transhipment of dangerous cargoes.

In Europe, under the EC Monitoring Directive, ports must provide a point of notification for dangerous or polluting goods on board ships. This duty differs from being the competent authority. Whoever is the person designated as the point of notification has the task of collecting and processing the obligatory dangerous cargo notifications.

Harbour Masters are frequently appointed as the competent authority in the enforcement of port maritime and nautical legislation and therefore may have police powers. Powers that they exercise in the enforcement of laws or port byelaws may include providing inspection services. The control of dangerous maritime goods and cargoes onboard ship and the handling of such goods in port terminals is a very important and highly specialised task of the Harbour Master's office. Even if they do not have police powers they will supervise the port to enforce the highest possible safety levels.

Some countries give port state control duties to Harbour Masters. And they may even be the authority which decides upon a vessel's detention; at the very least they will act in an advisory role when detentions are debated.

Statutory role: the authority		The ship-shore interface	
Rules, regulations and enforcement	**Nautical safety and port environment**	**Port operations and marine services**	**Specialist support in port development and management**
Admission to port: Port byelaws; admissions policy; point of notification	**Port safety:** Safety management and risk assessment; emergency response; ports of refuge; accident investigation	**Port marine operations:** navigation; planning port operations; port maintenance	**Port management:** Strategic planning; port engineering and equipment; nautical infrastructure
Inspections and enforcement: Port state control; detention of vessels; enforcement	**Vessel traffic services:** Traffic control; aids to navigation	**Port approach and fairways:** Dredging; deep water routes, traffic separation schemes; anchoring areas; hydrographic services; operation of bridges and locks	**Training and education:** Qualifications
Dangerous goods authority: Legislation; control of hazardous and noxious goods; LNG	**Port information:** Nautical port information; e-maritime and e-navigation; PCS	**Nautical technical services:** Pilotage; tug operations; mooring operations	**Other authorities in the port:** Port state control; health authority; customs
	Port environment: Pollution prevention and control; oil spill response; ship waste and ballast water; ships' emissions	**Terminals and cargo operations**	**Local community:** leisure use; high speed craft
	Port security: PSO, PFSO	**Ships' stay in port:** Bunkering; lashing tank cleaning; stores and crew	
		Port administration: Fee collection; statistics	

The authority: nautical safety and the port environment

The work of the Harbour Master is all about managing risks. With good risk management they will provide a safe port. This includes safety of navigation and port operations and the protection of the marine environment. In the last ten years, port security has also been added to the list of tasks.

Vessel traffic services (VTS) is a major risk control option for safe navigation. VTS is provided in maritime straits with dense traffic, along national coastlines and in ports where vessels are likely to be at close quarters. The responsibility for aids to navigation in port approaches and coastal areas usually rests with a national maritime authority, but in port areas it may rest with port authorities or Harbour Masters.

Accident prevention is a prime responsibility in the management of shipping. Nevertheless accidents may happen. Harbour Masters have a leading role in such port-related crises which may include collisions, explosions or the discharge of pollutants. They often have specific legal powers to act in such emergencies. Harbour Masters assist in crisis management and provide emergency response services. They may have an organisation in place for emergency response that cooperates with fire brigades, policy and health services. Firefighting capacity may be organised onboard patrol vessels, but may also be contracted by the port to a towage company.

Harbour Masters are often involved in accident investigation and may have a legal obligation to provide a port of refuge to vessels in distress as well as organising their passage to a safe harbour.

Often Harbour Masters are given a leading role in providing a sound port environment, taking care of pollution prevention and control. They may have an oil spill response organisation in place. Waste management services in ports, including the disposal of dangerous chemicals, may be strictly controlled by the Harbour Master to ensure compliance with all relevant laws and regulations. Harbour Masters, at least in Europe, may be a point of notification for the EU Directive on port reception facilities for ship-generated waste and cargo residues. They may be the body, designated by the national government, to collate all information that is to be provided before port entry on the issue of waste management.

In order to ensure port security, they may be the designated authority as defined by the ISPS Code. Under this Code a body, appointed by the national authority or by the competent authority for maritime security, must execute the tasks specified in EC regulations on enhancing ship and port facility security.

In the US, Harbour Masters, or their equivalent, coordinate salvage plans from vessels, in the event that there is a casualty in the port or port environs. This is under the auspices of OPA 90 Vessel Response Plan (VRP) requirements. The US Coast Guard states that VRPs should be activated when the Master of the vessel has determined that the response resources and personnel available on board cannot meet the needs of an actual or potential incident. The VRP may be activated by the vessel 'qualified individual' or vessel

Master, but the Captain of the Port may also direct VRP activation, if they determine such action is warranted but has not been undertaken.

Finally, they increasingly have a task in information management, providing port information or contributing to a port community system.

The ship-shore interface: port operations and marine services

So far the Harbour Master has been defined in terms of the authority in the port. But Harbour Masters are also involved in many other port marine operations and services. These include port operations planning or port maintenance.

For instance, their responsibilities in the port approaches and fairways may include dredging, setting dredging regimes or controlling dredging operations. They will advise on aids to navigation, on deep water routes, on traffic separation schemes and on the use of anchorages. They may support hydrographic services and regulate and oversee the operation of locks and bridges.

Another important aspect of the Harbour Master role may encompass marine technical services supplied to ships. These include the provision of pilotage, tug and mooring operations. When these services are offered by independent organisations, Harbour Masters still have a role in defining the standards for their provision, so that they will be delivered as a public service, that is, continuously to all port customers, regardless of size or status. These users will expect equal treatment and Harbour Masters will have to negotiate agreements reflecting these demands with marine technical service providers.

Harbour Masters are less and less involved directly in terminal and cargo operations as terminals are privatised. However, there are plenty of occasions during ships' stay in port, when advice from Harbour Masters is sought. This will be the case with services delivered by companies, organisations or government officials such as lashing services, fuel bunkering, tank cleaning and the delivery of stores, water and crew.

Harbour Masters may also have a role in the administration of ports, and be required to collect fees or statistics.

The ship-shore interface: support in port development and management

Harbour Masters do not exercise their profession in isolation; port managements, for example, may need advice in the strategic planning process, in port engineering and equipment provision or in development of the marine infrastructure.

There are usually channels for coordination with the port authority and Harbour Masters may also be represented within the governance structure of port authorities or be members of supervisory boards.

They may be involved in training and education, either for their own personnel or for those delivering services to the ship.

They have a role to play in the contacts with numerous authorities within the port such as port state control, health authorities and Customs.

Finally they deal with the local community so that ports, cities and local communities work in harmony. Operating a port, however safely it is done, always carries with it a certain risk to the population and to the habitat. Communities are quite aware of this vulnerability and do not hesitate to call upon the port to justify its actions.

Conclusion

It takes a lot to describe all the elements that could make up the Harbour Master's job. Harbour Masters develop their skills over many years and have to realise that they take sole responsibility for their actions. Harbour Masters have to take tough decisions taking into consideration the needs of everyone involved whether that includes governments, boards, shipowners or, indeed, their own employees. It is a responsibility that cannot be taken lightly.

A Harbour Master has to be everything to everybody. This book will serve to help explain some of the more common activities that Harbour Masters can be expected to face.

Ingrid Römers
Secretary European Harbour Masters Association
Senior Advisor Harbour Master Division Port of Rotterdam Authority

ABOUT THE AUTHOR

From the early 1980s Ingrid set up her own publishing house specialising in import/export trade publications. In the mid 1990s she moved to Rotterdam, working in a consulting company, undertaking the project management for business development projects in Eastern Europe.

In 2003 she moved to the Port of Rotterdam as Senior Advisor in the Harbour Masters' division, additionally taking, with pleasure, the role of Secretary of the EHMC. Ingrid has worked with the IHMA in several projects, including the website redevelopment, the Nautical Port Information project, the IHMA brochure and supporting the IHMA Development Officer. She has a degree in International Economics and Business from Erasmus University, Rotterdam with a minor in Maritime and Port Economics.

Chapter 2

The Harbour Master and the port approach area

By **Alan Coghlan**, President of the International Harbour Masters' Association

Introduction

This chapter deals with navigational problems and relations with other bodies in the area of port approaches. When addressing this issue, it is hard not to rely on my own experience as it applies to the port at which I have been Harbour Master. Appreciating this, I have tried to cater for most types of ports, having taken note that they exist in many different environments and there is no standard location or typical port.

For example there are ports located on the coast, within an estuary or within the jurisdiction of other ports or authorities, which can present unique problems in ensuring the safety of the approach to a specific port.

Balancing safety with commercial wellbeing

Safety is the main concern of Harbour Masters and in particular the safety of their principal customers: the ships using their port. To that end a Harbour Master must be satisfied that all stages of the passage from the sea to the port are the safest possible for all the ships calling there.

Principal concerns will centre on:

- Available depths
- Lighting and marking of the channel
- Alignment of the channel
- Tidal regime
- Meteorological conditions
- Coastal VTS
- Anchorages
- Physical restriction or pinch points
- The availability of pilots to suit the needs of the port

Another problem exists and it is nothing the Harbour Master directly controls. That is the perceived decline in the standard of seamanship on a minority of vessels calling into ports. Because of this, and all of the other factors mentioned, Harbour Masters must be satisfied that their approach channel is as safe as practicable without involving excessive expenditure. This is a problem for all Harbour Masters, no matter the location, the size of port, the nature of the trade or the type of ship.

If we look the list of factors that influence the port approach and those bodies that, apart from the port, control each of the factors (Table 1.1 below). The Harbour Master has to consider how to interact with each of those bodies to achieve the optimum balance between safety and the commercial wellbeing of the port.

1.1 Factors that influence the port approach and controlling bodies

Factor	Issue	Controlling body
Coastal navigation	Restricted access	National administration
Pilotage	Delays	Pilotage authority or port company
Coastal VTS	Adequacy of control	National administration
Anchorages	Suitability	Port company
Aids to navigation	Adequacy for 24 hour access	National lighthouse authority
Depths	Sufficient depth for all dynamic operations	National administration and/or port company
Port entrance	Design	Third party port or own port company

Jurisdiction issues

If you are lucky enough to work in a port whose jurisdiction extends to the coast and the open sea, the number of external factors and controlling bodies are greatly diminished. But the problems do not go away. One simply has to deal with them oneself rather than relying on others. Working in a port or jurisdiction in which pilots are employed or licensed by that port, there is a great opportunity to interact directly with the pilots rather than through a controlling body.

But working in a port which is situated within the jurisdiction of another, and there are hundreds of examples, most of the problems lie with someone else upon whom you must rely to achieve the optimum balance for your port.

So what are the issues and problems that are of concern? Let us examine some of them and identify the bodies that may be responsible for them in your jurisdiction:

Formal risk assessment

Starting from the open sea and the coastal area in the vicinity of the port, this is the area directly controlled by the national administration of the particular coastal state. Your port may be situated close to busy shipping lanes, with the added restriction of deep water routes, controlled by coastal VTS. The presence of deep water routes and traffic separation schemes (TSS) may restrict access to your port for other vessels. Or perhaps the lack of such a route may hamper development plans envisaged for your port. As with any issue about safety that arises, and in this case, it is the safety of shipping within the approach to your port that is in question, the only empirical measurement of the risk involved is by a formal risk assessment.

Pilotage

Having examined the coastal element, we should look at the adequacy of the pilot boarding area for the size of ship using your port.

- Is it a very busy area?
- Does the pilotage authority have a sufficient number of pilots to prevent delays?
- Are some pilotage exemptions in force?
- How do piloted and non-piloted ships interact?

The pilot boarding area is one where the greatest danger to a ship exists, especially if the area is not properly controlled. This is particularly true where the area is very busy and where there is a strong current across the entrance. The relevant questions are:

- Is this area controlled by VTS?
- If so, who operates and controls the system?
- What sort of service is offered?

Aids to navigation

Dealing with channel marking and lighting, the questions that come to mind are simple enough:

- Is the channel adequately buoyed for the range of vessels calling to your port?
- Is the channel properly lit to allow 24 hour access for the range of vessels?
- Are there sufficient shore marks and lights such as leading lights?
- Do you as a port company have the right to independently establish lights or buoys etc. without seeking sanction from a central controlling body?

The Nautical Institute's book *The Use of Visual Aids to Navigation*, second edition, gives background to the importance to these.

Anchorage

With anchorages the obvious questions include:

- Are they safe enough to provide shelter in bad weather?
- Is the holding ground sufficient for all ships in all tidal conditions?
- Is the anchorage monitored and, if so, by whom?
- How is the anchorage portrayed on the chart, eg by a large box or definite positions for different sized ships?
- Are there specific areas for ships with hazardous cargoes to anchor?
- Is the anchorage close to the pilot station?

Navigable channels

These must be examined as they are the actual channels to your own port entrance. If the channel lies within the jurisdiction of another body it is your duty, as Harbour Master, to ensure the channel has an adequate depth and width for the maximum size of vessel that will use your port. Or to put it another way, decide the actual maximum size of vessel you will accept even in the face of commercial pressure.

Another important factor to consider in examining this issue is the direction of the currents in relation to the direction of the channel. I would recommend the *PIANC Study on Channel Design* to establish whether there are issues in relation to the design of your approach channel.

Plan ahead

So far I have listed a series of questions. I recommend that you ask yourself these questions about the approach to your port. This is a very basic form of risk assessment. As previously touched upon, the only empirical method of establishing the degree of risk is an actual formal risk assessment. It is valid for you to risk assess the approach to your port, whether you control the approach or not. Alternatively you may choose to employ the services of a marine expert in such studies to have the work carried out. Beyond that I do not recommend you proceed until you have formally approached all the bodies which control the various factors affecting the safety of the approach channel.

It is important to realise that, without the cooperation of these various bodies, improvements in the safety of an approach channel cannot be achieved. At the very least it will be extremely difficult. Each of the bodies identified performs independent and important functions but significantly it is within or at a port entrance that all the bodies meet or overlap. The national lighthouse authority, the pilotage authority for the area, the national authority, to a lesser degree, and the port all share a common interface at the port entrance and within the port. More importantly each is concerned with the safety of the ship and the prevention of a disaster.

Find out, through an informal approach in the first instance who, within each of the bodies, is the correct person to deal with as each of these bodies has statutory functions, including the port. Bring your concerns and results of risk assessment to them before making the formal approach. All successful problem resolution is better facilitated through initial personal contact and developing trust.

Following the initial contact, a more formal approach must follow that outlines the problems you have identified and, where necessary, producing the risk assessment as evidence of those problems. Ideally, all the stakeholders of whom we have been talking should be encouraged to make concrete contributions to greatly mitigate the risks identified. It is vital that they are part of the solution because, as stated previously, without the goodwill and cooperation of those bodies your port will not develop as it should.

Planning considerations

Harbour Masters must also be conscious of future trends, particularly the increasing size of ships. In this commercial world, we must plan for the future in anticipation of developments in shipping.

When considering plans for the future development of a port, the Harbour Master must also be aware of a new international trend in the generation of power for domestic and industrial consumption. I refer of course to renewable energy using wind, tidal and wave generators. The drive for sustainable renewable energy is very desirable and understandable. Of necessity, these devices must be deployed close to the shore for ease of access to facilitate maintenance and also for proximity to the national power grid to facilitate cheaper recovery and distribution.

Ports are normally large centres of population with high energy demands. They have facilities in place to service the reception and deployment of units. And of course, they are close to national or regional grids, favourable locations for power generating industries. This may bring ports, the national administration and the power generation industry into conflict.

For the sake of clarity, a brief explanation of the methods currently used in power development, may be useful.

Wind

Everyone is by now familiar with the wind generating units referred to as windmills. They are normally large static structures standing some 40 metres in height with three 15 metre blades which are driven by the wind to generate electricity.

Waves

Wave generation is still largely in development but consists of a floating structure, which converts the energy of swell and waves into electric power. These units will be anchored off-shore but close to land for the ease of maintenance and power recovery.

Tides

Tidal or current generation uses the tidal flow to generate power. These units are generally some 10 metres in diameter and are fixed to the seabed, again close to the shore for ease of maintenance and power recovery.

Implications

We must consider how these units will affect port approaches and their safety. Port approaches have the greatest concentrations of ships waiting for, or disembarking, their pilots. So it is naturally the area where there will be the most incidents of ships at close quarters and where the greatest caution is required.

Planners who oversee the implementation and rollout of new renewable power schemes see the areas close to the coast and port approaches as being the natural areas in which to deploy the new technology. This deployment increases the danger to shipping in those approaches.

Some governments have granted rights to power companies to the edges of recognised shipping lanes and port approaches, without the provision of safe buffer zones. These will allow approaching vessels to take avoiding action which may necessitate leaving those recognised lanes in the interest of taking timely avoiding action. Such problems may include loss of engine power and anchoring temporarily outside those lanes. They might include an alteration of course to avoid crossing traffic thereby putting them into the areas reserved for renewable energy farms.

This is particularly the case in the future development or installation of wind farms. Any commercial developer will wish to maximise exploitation of the area granted to them, which may result in saturation of the complete area to the detriment of safe navigation.

There is a compelling argument to control the shape or physical layout of wind farms allowable in port approaches. In most cases a diamond shape may well be preferable to a block shape. This is particularly true where the point of a diamond shape coincides with an area of crossing traffic in a port approach. There is also a compelling argument to suggest the area of a port approach can be considered far greater than the immediate environs of the port itself. If there are perceived difficulties in the approach to a port over a greater distance then the shipowner and ship's Master might perceive that port to be difficult to access.

In the case of tidal energy recovery, the units are submerged and then become underwater obstructions to shipping. The same commercial logic will apply in terms of a developer wishing to maximise exploitation, which will have the same effect as that posed by wind farms. Commercial companies interested in such technology have already identified areas of high tidal or current energy and some of these areas are within ports and close to port approaches.

The most dangerous scenario occurs with the deployment of floating devices to harness wave motion and convert it into power. These units will be anchored to the seabed in specified areas. Given the need for high swell and wave action to make these units viable, the most worrying aspect of such technology is the inherent danger of breakout during periods of extreme weather. The units, which are large enough to cause damage even to the largest ship, could wreak havoc with shipping in the approaches to a port. If there were a large scale breakout or dragging across port approaches there may well be a port closure until all units have been recovered.

The big problem for Harbour Masters is that the areas likely to be chosen for such developments, or those already in place, are outside a Harbour Master's area of jurisdiction. Therefore they normally are not consulted about such developments, as those granting rights sometimes do not fully appreciate the far-reaching effect of the licenses granted.

We cannot be against such developments as they obviously are of such great benefit to the communities in which we operate and are of such great benefit to the environment in which we all live. That said we cannot allow situations to develop close to our ports that would in any way restrict or impair access to a port.

The Future.

There is a need a best-practice guide for development close to port approaches. I would like to think that IHMA could develop that and that this would be seen as a beneficial contribution. But this is a discussion for the future.

Captain Alan Coghlan

ABOUT THE AUTHOR

Alan went to sea in 1966 and was promoted to Captain in 1979. In 1982 he came ashore to work with The Limerick Harbour Commissioners. After 11 years as Assistant Harbour Master he was promoted to Harbour Master of the Shannon Estuary and served in that position for 18 years. During that time there were many corporate changes including an amalgamation of the two ports on the estuary. Alan has extensive experience in pilotage, towage handling of large vessels and working vessels in high current velocities. He retired as Harbour Master in 2011.

Alan has been involved with the IHMA since 1994, serving as Chairman of the Papers Committee, and as President following his election at the Malta Congress in 2006.

image: Fotolia

Chapter 3

Maritime port and terminal information

By **Captain Ing Ben van Scherpenzeel**

Why should we, as professionals, have to work with unprofessional information? That's a question often heard within the maritime industry.

Compared to making a hotel reservation, booking a terminal berth is not as straightforward. It's indeed a strange state of affairs. If one wants to book a hotel room worth $250 and drive up to that hotel in a car worth $15,000, that poses no difficulty; one gets all the desired details by a few clicks on the internet.

But when one wants to book a terminal berth, worth billions, sailing to it with a vessel loaded with a cargo totalling perhaps $100 million, it's very difficult to obtain reliable information.

And this begs the question, why?

Perhaps it is because only a very few people understand that all parties involved need reliable information. It might be that even fewer people understand that those parties provide different and possibly conflicting, information. This could lead to reduced safety and increased inefficiencies in the nautical chain of loading a cargo into a vessel and bringing it to its destination.

The dilemma is simple. If a ship is loaded, discharged, operated and serviced by people who all have different information about the same ports, there will always be errors. If the Master of a ship is required to navigate with a selection of different and conflicting sets of charts and nautical publications, there would be maritime chaos.

Thus the starting point is that port information must come from one source, must be reliable and must have a format that serves all parties.

Maritime port information: from pilot station to the berth; Harbour Masters are seen as the authoritative and trusted source for port information.

Terminal information: from the berth to the terminal gate; information is provided by the terminal operator.

Both sources of information are needed by all parties. They are required by cargo owners, by Shipmasters and the maritime service providers, including the appointed ship's agent.

Initially we should study these parties and their respective responsibilities, what information they require and why.

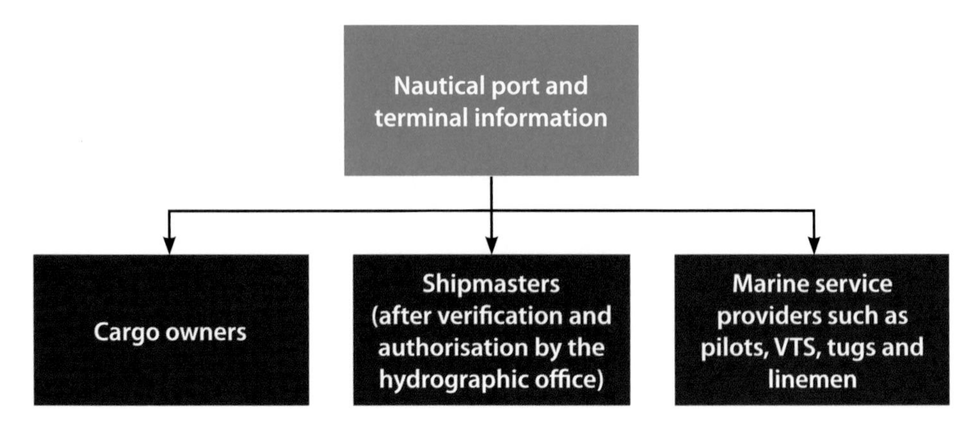

3.1 The need for port information

Cargo owners

Cargo owners put cargo into vessels, which may be owned or chartered. They check if the vessels can sail safely to terminals and perform cargo operations. They need confirmation that the vessel can sail safely up to the berth at the terminal, handle a specified amount of cargo and sail again. To make these judgments, cargo owners need maritime port information.

In the tanker sector for instance, all parties will realise that a one centimetre difference in loaded draft may result in as much as a 90 tonne margin for a medium sized tanker such as an aframax. Unreliable charted depth and tidal information can result in an extra safety margin being applied to gain a required under keel clearance. This is a considerable reduction in cargo. The trend is for ships to increase in size, so ports have to strictly apply safety margins. Thus accurate information on approaches, fairways, buoyage, berthing and terminals is essential.

In the tanker sector, further restrictions have to be factored in. The manifold of the tanker must fit with the manifold of the terminal at all states of the tide. The rise and fall of the vessel as its draught increases or decreases as a result of cargo operations must be considered. At some tanker berths, the vessel can only come alongside if its minimum parallel body length matches the distance between breasting dolphins.

Masters

Cargo owners must determine that vessels, in ballast or with a certain amount of cargo on board, can sail to the terminal and perform berthing and cargo operations safely and efficiently. A plan is then made in conjunction with terminal officials. This plan and the location and position of the terminal are sent to the Master of the vessel with what are termed cargo orders.

After receiving these orders the Master must make a mandatory voyage plan. Masters must comply with the IMO requirements for berth to berth passage planning. That this is an essential tool is highlighted by maritime accidents statistics that show that most occur between the pilot station and the berth. In accordance with SOLAS Chapter V, the Captain should use official and compliant information for voyage and passage planning. This is information that has been verified and authorised by a hydrographic office. These, in their turn, rely on input from port authorities, as coastal areas are subject to greater physical change than the oceans. Information from deep sea areas is collected by survey vessels employed by national hydrographic offices for the relevant exclusive economic zones (EEZ). Areas not covered by national hydrographic offices are continually surveyed by vessels from the UK Hydrographic Office.

For planning purposes, the Master needs accurate tidal details in order to calculate the optimum time of arrival at the pilot station or berth. Certain terminals might have a tidal window and it makes little sense to arrive at a pilot station at a time that does not coincide with this window.

Terminal information is needed and is usually confirmed by the ship's agent, as the Master needs to be sure that the berth is available before the pilot boards. The significance of planning the vessel's speed and accurate ETA is highlighted by the fact that a small decrease in engine speed has a huge impact on bunker consumption, which makes up 70% of the vessel's running costs.

Additionally, there is a drive to reduce greenhouse gas emissions at sea. By sailing to the pilot station at an economic (low) speed with proper maritime port and terminal information, a vessel can save up to 50% of its normal bunker consumption.

Apart from voyage planning, the Master needs to prepare for berthing and cargo operations once the vessel is in port. For mooring the Master needs information such as positions and safe working loads of bollards or hooks. For cargo operations the Master needs to know the diameter and position of the cargo manifold, or the position of cranes. If the Master is able to prepare the vessel properly, it makes the berthing and cargo handling process much more safe and efficient.

Nautical service providers

When the Master arrives off the port, the vessel is assisted by maritime service providers. These include the VTS operator, the pilot, the tugs and linemen. Apart from VTS, all these services are booked by the ship's agent.

Based on port and terminal information, the VTS operator will advise the Master to proceed or to wait at the anchorage. Here, port information such as tidal windows is important to confirm berth availability.

If the VTS operator allows the vessel to enter the port, the ship will steam up to the pilot station where the pilot will board. The pilot and Master will confer, discussing the passage between pilot station and the terminal. This is the final part of the passage plan. They will discuss the number of tugs and the mooring arrangements. Apart from the prevailing weather conditions which will affect mooring operations, much of what is required is held in port and terminal information records.

Maritime port information is consulted for such things as speed restrictions and rendezvous points for tugs. Terminal information is needed for such things as berthing requirements and restrictions.

Once the pilot is on board the vessel proceeds into the port. The next operation will be making fast the tugs. Both the crew of the tug and the crew of the vessel need to be standing by on deck to connect the towing line with the vessel. Once connected, this operation needs to be monitored. Only if Masters knows the tug rendezvous point will they be able to give the crew sufficient notice to standby.

Finally the vessel arrives at the terminal, where linemen will assist the crew to moor up the vessel. Linemen need to know ahead of time which line will go where, avoiding needless discussions with the crew of the vessel on arrival.

These ship operations underline the importance of all parties, cargo owners, the charterers, the Masters and maritime service providers, having access to the same information.

We should now study why all these concerned parties don't have the same information.

Cargo owners get their information from mainly unauthorised sources: for example from websites of ports and terminals; port and terminal information booklets or flyers; ship's agents and private databases. All these information sources may differ from source to source, be presented in differing formats, might not be available in English or maybe poorly translated.

To update private databases, many cargo owners send out questionnaires to ports and terminals. However these questionnaires are not consistent. Completing them is administratively cumbersome, resource intensive and leads to differing information about the same port or terminal. So it's no surprise that cargo owners are confused.

The Master may only work navigationally with official and compliant information from hydrographic offices and their nautical charts and books. However some marine charts and books are now being updated via questionnaires. So Masters, in the same way as cargo owners, do not necessarily get reliable information to amend their nautical publications.

Maritime service providers all use their own information. VTS operators use their own manuals, which may differ from the other service providers such as pilots.

It is therefore apparent that port and terminal information must be accurate, consistent, up-to-date and comprehensive. Quite simply, all parties must be singing from the same hymn sheet.

Firstly it should be presented in such a way that cargo owners, hydrographic offices which publish charts and books for the Shipmaster, and maritime service providers can work with it. Secondly, information should be exchanged digitally so it's up to date. Apart from this, vessels are using more and more digital charts and books, requiring more frequent digital updates.

For both maritime port and terminal information, a solution has now been found and is being applied. For port information, the IHMA has worked closely with cargo owners, hydrographic offices and maritime service providers. This cooperation has resulted in two standardised formats to provide information in a uniform way.

One template is for general maritime port information, the Port Information Guide.

A second template covers specific port information, the Port Sections Guide with corresponding charts, photographs, soundings and pilot passage plans.

3.2 IHMA information guides are easily recognised by these logos

General nautical port information applies to the whole port area and provides the following information via the *Port Information Guide*:

- Introduction, contact information and regulations
- Notification, documentation and reporting
- Port description and navigation
- Port safety and security
- Nautical services and communication
- Cargo operations
- Vessel operations

Many ports have already completed the Port Information Guide; the information is published at www.harbourmaster.org Their experiences are being used to fine-tune the template and expand details in this book.

In the Port Section Guide, specific nautical port information is included to describe each section of the port: For example, ports approaches, the anchorage, the pilot station, port entrance, rivers or canals, bridges and locks, basins and berths, together with information about the depth and policy alongside. It holds information necessary for arrivals such as UKC policy, restrictions, passing requirements, tug use, berthing requirements. It also has information for departures, which is often similar as that for arrivals.

In addition to this Port Sections Guide, there are charts, photographs, soundings and pilot passage plans being provided for relevant sections.

3.3 IHMA *Port Information Guides*

The Oil Companies International Marine Forum (OCIMF) was the first to address the need for information on wet terminals through its Marine terminal particulars questionnaire – a uniform digital questionnaire for all wet bulk terminals. In 2012 this project was in its start-up phase. Marine terminal information is provided in a standard format. The terminal can share this information with the cargo owner, the Shipmaster and maritime service providers, including the ship's agent. The questionnaire provides information such as mooring plan information, maximum sizes per berth, manifold information, safety information, etc.

For other types of terminal, a solution has not yet been found.

	Port Sections Guide
	Sections 58
	Read user guidelines first. Always check all adjoining sections
Port	**Rotterdam**
Section	**1e Petroleumhaven**
Date	**21-12-2010**
Position (lat / lon)	51°53'.2N 004°20'.8E
Minimum control-led water depth	See section chart
Chart datum	See section chart
Range of water densities	Mean: 999 kg/m^3, Min: 998 kg/m3, Max: 1001 kg/m^3
Tidal range	Mean range: 1.73m
UKC policy alongside	Always afloat, UKC recommended 0,30 meter
Bottom type	Mix of mud and silt. Mix rate depends on tidal situation.
Dredging regime	
Distance pilot station to berth	From Racon Maascenter Bouy 52° 00'.9N 002° 48'.8E : 13.3Nm
ISPS	
Loading/unloading requirements	
Free text	
Manoeuvre	**Arrival**
UKC policy	UKC = 0,50 meter.
Size restriction	
Tidal restriction	**L≥200 m and T < 10.8 m:** During slack water high tide = HWR +1.15 or slack water low tide = HWR - 2.30 **T≥10.8 m:** During slack at HW = HWR + 1.15
Wind restriction	
Visibility restriction	
Speed restriction	
Passing requirements	
Tug use	Rendezvous point close to 51°55'.0N 004°15'.0E
Berthing requirements	
Free text option	
Manoeuvre	**Departure**
UKC policy	UKC = 0,50 meter.
Size restriction	
Tidal restriction	**L≥200 m:** HWR +1.15 till HWR -2.30
Wind restriction	
Visibility restriction	
Speed restriction	
Passing requirements	
Tug use	

3.4 Example of a Port Sections Guide

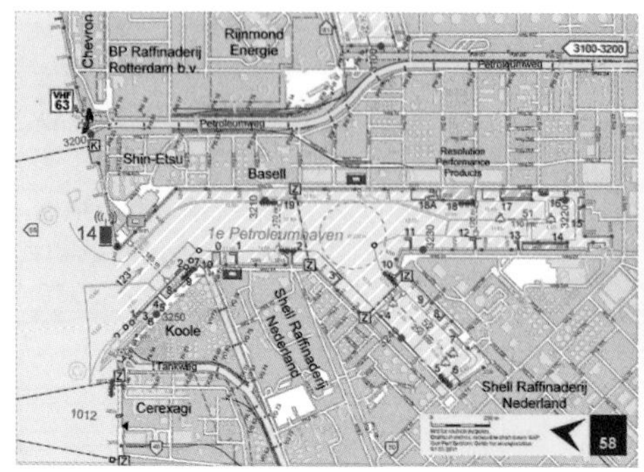

3.5 Port section chart, with information including minimum controlled water depth, chart datum, name of terminals

3.6 Port section photo

Rotterdam Pilot Station →Petroleumhaven No: 1

No	Waypoint Name	Waypoint Position		Direction	Distance between waypoints(nm)	Distance from Pilotstation(nm)
1	Rotterdam Pilot Station	51-59.0 N	003-47.2 E			
				082	7.9	
2	MVN	52-00.1 N	004-00.0 E			7.9
				112	1.3	
3	Maas 1	51-59.6 N	004-02.0 E			9.2
				107	2.6	
4	NW-9	51-58.8 N	004-06.0 E			11.8
				114	0.8	
5	Hoek van Holland	51-58.5 N	004-07.2 E			12.6
				124	0.9	
6	Viandasteiger	51-58.0 N	004-08.4 E			13.5
				131	1.7	
7	Bn-11	51-56.9 N	004-10.5 E			15.2
				124	0.6	
8	Bn-13	51-56.6 N	004-11.3 E			15.8
				119	0.7	
9	NW-21	51-56.2 N	004-12.3 E			16.5
				123	0.4	
10	Bn-18	51-56.0 N	004-12.9 E			16.9
				136	0.5	
11	Bn-21	51-55.6 N	004-13.5 E			17.4
				142	0.6	
12	Bn-25	51-55.1 N	004-14.1 E			18
				133	0.4	
13	Maassluis	51-54.8 N	004-14.6 E			18.4
				122	1.7	
14	Bn-37	51-53.9 N	004-17.0 E			20.1
				104	1	
15	Botlek	51-53.7 N	004-18.5 E			21.1
				097	0.6	
16	Oude Maas	51-53.6 N	004-19.5 E			21.7
				083	0.7	
17	Petroleumhaven no: 1	51-53.7 N	004-20.5 E			22.4

3.7 Port Section Pilot Passage Plan with courses, distances etc

3.8 The relationship between the different international projects

Type of information	Source of information	Product	Project leader	Status
General maritime port information	Harbour Master	Port Information Guide	IHMA	Template accepted and completed by 12 ports; input for web version
Specific maritime port information	Harbour Master	Port Sections Guide	IHMA	Template accepted and completed by one port
Port electronic navigational chart (ENC)	National hydrographic offices	Port ECN	National hydrographic offices	Work in progress (at 2012). Input from ports is still an issue
Marine terminal information	Terminal operator	Marine terminal particulars questionnaire	OCIMF	Final template tested in several terminals
Pilot passage plan	Pilots	Pilot passage plan	Local pilot organisation	In place in Australian and European ports

Only by providing comprehensive and reliable nautical port and terminal information, preferably in digital format, to cargo owners, Shipmasters and marine, nautical and maritime service providers, can we improve safety and efficiency in the commercial maritime chain.

Captain Ing Ben van Scherpenzeel

Director nautical developments, policy and plans Port of Rotterdam

Ben was born in Maarssen in the centre of Holland, and was educated at the Nautical Academy in Terschelling, one of the Netherland's northern islands. After his graduation in 1990, he started as a third officer with Shell Tankers and Seatrade. In 1993 he joined Holland America Line and worked for 12 years as a deck officer, staff captain and project manager of newbuild programmes.

He joined the Port of Rotterdam in 2004. His responsibilities are the development of nautical information applications; new planning and reporting schemes for vessels; mooring systems and maritime spatial planning for the North Sea.

In addition to his assignment at the Port of Rotterdam, Ben is also project leader for the IHMA and the EHMC.

Together with EHMC secretary Ingrid Römers, author of Chapter 1 and Chapter 17, he developed the Nautical Port Information Project and videos such as *The Chain* and *The Missing Link*.

During his holidays he loves to explore the Dutch waters in Holland on boats smaller than those he served at sea on, to dock at a waterside restaurant to enjoy a good meal, with a good glass of wine, nice music and fun company.

Chapter 4

The Harbour Master and vessel traffic services

By **Jillian Carson-Jackson** M Ed MNI AFRIN

Vessel traffic services (VTS) can be a valuable tool to ensure safe, effective and efficient movement of vessels in ports. VTS can also be developed to assist coastal vessel transits. This chapter will present key components of VTS, including the need to ensure that successful legislation is in place to support operations. It identifies different equipment for operations, the personnel elements of running a VTS and explains what it can, and cannot, offer.

An overview of VTS

VTS has its roots in the mid 1900s. In 1946 the then Admiralty of Great Britain worked with the then Mersey Docks and Harbour Board to carry out experiments with naval radar equipment on the shore at Liverpool. The demonstration was a success and similar experiments were carried out in Southampton in the UK, Halifax in Canada, Le Havre in France and Long Beach in the USA. These lead to several resolutions and guidelines from the International Maritime Organization (IMO) starting in 1968, then in 1985 and 1997.

The International Association of Marine Aids to Navigation and Lighthouse Authorities (IALA) recognises the importance of VTS services. Its VTS Manual states: 'The realities of modern shipping, with larger and less manoeuvrable ships, traffic congestion in ports, hazardous cargoes and the potential for environmental damage, demand that sophisticated measures be taken to reduce risks. Establishing a VTS is a significant response to that demand. When established, implemented and operated within the context of international laws, conventions and maritime customs, and with the cooperation of vessel operators, a VTS can contribute substantially to the safety and efficiency of maritime traffic and protection of the environment'.

Legislation and related documentation

The legislative aspects of VTS rest in international conventions; international documentation on best practice in VTS, national acts and laws and local or municipal regulation. Each VTS will need to respond to the legislative aspects in a manner which addresses the unique environment it operates in.

An overview of VTS related documentation is provided at www.nautinst.org/TWOTHM

International level

Ship reporting is referenced in different IMO conventions. The IALA has also developed a significant body of work that represents international best practice in the development and implementation of VTS.

VTS are specifically referenced in the IMO SOLAS Convention, Chapter V, Regulation 12. In addition, Regulation 11, *Ship Reporting Systems*, may also be of relevance to the implementation of VTS that extends beyond territorial waters. Resolution A.857(20) provides guidance on development, implementation and operation of the service. The Manilla Amendments to the STCW Convention reference a need to include training for ship personnel on VTS. Communication aspects of VTS are included in the IMO Standard Navigational Communication Phrases (SMCP).

The IALA membership has significant experience in the development, implementation and subsequent operation of VTS. The IALA VTS Committee meets twice each year, and IALA hosts a targeted VTS Symposium every four years.

National/local levels

At both the IMO and IALA level there is recognition of the need to ensure effective legislation and policy at the national and local level to enable effective implementation of VTS.

The manner in which this is addressed will depend on the unique port location, local and national legislation and the level of service that the VTS should provide in those circumstances. VTS cannot be effective without the appropriate level of legislation to empower the operation.

Legislation may also exist for some element of Harbour Master powers which could include:

- Scheduling of vessel movements and the times between which a vessel may transit
- Implementation and monitoring of speed limits
- Movement restricted areas
- One-way routes and the assigning of anchorages
- Incident response
- Interaction with other services within the port

VTS operators could be a means to respond to some, or all, of these obligations depending on the approach taken within the port.

Levels of service

IMO identifies three service aspects for VTS:

Information service (INS) – ensures essential information becomes available in time for onboard navigational decision-making

Traffic organisation service (TOS) – prevents the development of dangerous maritime traffic situations and provides for the safe and efficient movement of vessel traffic within the VTS area

Navigational assistance service (NAS) – assists onboard navigational decision-making and monitors its effects

The IALA VTS manual expands on the concept, noting that the basic service level is an information service, but the levels are not hierarchal and each may exist in specified areas of a VTS service.

Local port service (LPS) has been developed to respond to the practical instances where a risk analysis has not identified the need for a VTS, but where specific services are provided to ensure the smooth operation of the port. It is a shore organisation that only provides information to the bridge team and does not interact in any way with traffic. An LPS is designed to improve port safety and coordination of port services by the dissemination of port information to vessels and berth or terminal operators. It is mainly concerned with the management of the port. As it is not a VTS, LPS are not required to have the ability and or the resources to maintain a traffic image or respond to developing traffic situations. In addition, personnel will not be trained to the same level as VTS personnel. LPS and each of the VTS service levels are explained in detail in Chapter 5, *IALA VTS Manual* (2008).

VTS – an information hub

VTS normally operates on a 24/7 roster and can be seen as a focal point for information exchange within a port. Through the linking of technical systems, operational processes and trained, professional VTS personnel, VTS is an information hub for the port.

Working with many allied services, which may include pilotage; ship agents; port state control; cargo and passenger transfers and agents; VTS provides benefits to the overall efficiency and safety of the port. For a Harbour Master, this one stop shop for timely information on port activities, both receipt and dissemination, adds a further layer in overall port operations.

The role of VTS as a first responder in incidents means that careful consideration must be taken in developing contingency plans for the port and providing training for VTS personnel. A clear initial response and call-out procedure for the VTS officer (VTSO) can greatly enhance the overall response. The converse is also true, where the VTS is not clearly integrated into the port response then the benefit of the service can be lost and may actually hinder operations through duplication of effort.

Determining the need for VTS

As noted in the IMO SOLAS regulation, the level of risk or volume of traffic is assessed to justify implementing a VTS. The need for the VTS is usually determined as part of an overall risk assessment process for the port. Some examples of why a VTS may be required include:

- Protection of the environment
- Protection of port infrastructure
- Enhanced efficiency of ship movements
- Focus monitoring of conflict area including pilot boarding grounds, dredging activities or port development activities

Maritime security

Two key questions that need to be asked when determining the need for a VTS are:

1) What are the environmental, safety and economic consequences of having or not having a VTS?

2) What is the level of investment and cost benefit that can be justified by implementing a VTS?

The cost benefit analysis of a VTS is explained in the *IALA VTS Manual*, which includes a flow chart for the steps that could be taken in determining the need for a VTS.

Resources for VTS

Implementing and operating a VTS is a significant investment in time, money and personnel. When addressing resources it is imperative to look not only at the start up costs for equipment and facilities, but also human resources, training and continuing costs associated with running a 24/7 operation.

Financial resources

At a financial level VTS costs can be linked to the start up costs, such as:

- Consulting
- Equipment installation and commissioning
- Facility costs for antennas, construction and communication lines
- Personnel costs: recruitment, training and retention
- Programme monitoring and assessment

The risk analysis that was carried out to determine the need for VTS will provide the basis for the cost/benefit analysis. When faced with a possible incident in a busy waterway or environmentally sensitive area the cost to lost productivity and clean up can significantly outweigh the cost for implementing and running a VTS.

Human resources

VTS is a service and the personnel delivering it play a key role in implementation and effecting operations. Requirements for personnel will depend on a number of elements, including:

- Area monitored – traffic density and environmental considerations
- Sensor capability
- Decision support tool capability
- Recruitment policies
- Training elements
- Recruitment

There have been many discussions about who to recruit to the role of a VTSO. In some areas there is a requirement for Master Mariner or some level of maritime experience, while in other areas high school leavers are recruited. VTS personnel are now recognised as maritime professionals, with a focus on job competencies rather than pre-requisites for intake levels.

Training

Training of VTS personnel is a critical element in ensuring effective service delivery. IALA has carried out considerable work regarding the training of VTSOs, producing generic recommendations and a series of model courses. The model courses are designed as outcomes; looking at the competencies required of a VTSO and then identifying a series of modules to verify these competencies.

The modular approach can be tailored to the intake level, for example, recruits with previous maritime experience may have reduced training time through a prior learning assessment approach. All VTS training requires on-the-job training to ensure competence in elements such as local knowledge, equipment and incident or contingency plan response.

Equipment

VTS needs to be able to maintain a traffic image and communicate with vessels. A VTS traffic image is defined as the surface picture of a vessel and its movements in a VTS area. IALA has recognised the importance of equipment within a VTS centre and has developed a series of documents related to equipment standards: V-128 on *Operational and Technical Performance Requirements for VTS Equipment*, with a series of annexes for specific equipment, including radar, AIS, radio-communications and CCTV.

The implementation, monitoring and maintenance of equipment associated with VTS plays a key role in effective service delivery.

Communication technologies

As an information hub, VTS relies on communication technologies. Communications within a VTS can include:

- VHF radio
- Telephone communications including mobile, fixed and satellite phones
- E-mail either fixed or by satellite
- Facsimile continues to be used, but e-mail is beginning to cover most elements of what would have been sent via fax
- Internet, including linked systems with allied services and the presentation of a common operational picture

Linked to communication technologies are procedures. Clearly identified standard operating procedures for all aspects of communications, including the use of the IMO SMCP VTS phrases, should be implemented in a VTS.

Sensors

Sensors are used to ensure VTS has the ability to create and maintain a traffic image. The significant development in sensor technology has enabled the addition of decision support tools to assist VTSO in assessing situations.

Sensors in VTS are geared to providing and maintaining a traffic image and can include:

- VHF voice reporting at set 'calling in points' (CIP) or for exceptional circumstances, report of detects or deficiencies
- Radar
- Automatic identification system (AIS)
- Close circuit television (CCTV)
- Satellite automatic position reporting (APR) for vessels in areas not covered by other sensors

Sensor information needs to be presented in a clear and unambiguous fashion to enable the VTSO to make best use of the data available. To do this, a number of single screens, integrated solutions have been developed. These include the ability to implement electronic 'corridors', alarm management, vessel grouping; for example, all tankers over a specific size and the linking of data with port management tools such as ship movement planning, berthing, logistics and finance systems.

Conclusion

VTS can provide an effective service to both port and ship operations. It is important that the role of VTS within a port or coastal waterway is clearly understood. This role has been highlighted in the IALA flyer *What a Shipmaster can expect of the VTS and what is expected of the Shipmaster* which can be found at www.iala-aism.org

The role of VTS needs to be clearly communicated with users and allied services, including specifics on:

Equipment

The communications and sensor coverage area, including the surveillance systems radar, AIS and CCTV. In addition, the decision making tools and any specifics such as close track monitoring areas, geographically 'fenced' areas for alerts and movement restriction areas.

Service levels

The type of service provided such as information service, navigational assistance service or traffic organisation service. This should include areas and times of operation if these services are not provided 24/7 throughout the full area.

Personnel

Entry levels and training provided for VTS personnel. Authorities should endeavour to ensure VTS personnel are trained to international standards for the type of service being provided.

Procedures

Established standard procedures that reflect the service level identified and ensure consistent interaction with port services and vessels operating in the coverage area need to be clearly documented and communicated to all parties. Procedures would include contingency planning for the port operations, and these need to be exercised regularly.

A VTS is another tool for effective port operations, and can be an integral element in the work of the Harbour Master.

Jillian Carson-Jackson M Ed MNI AFRIN

Manager, Vessel Tracking
Australian Maritime Safety Authority

ABOUT THE AUTHOR

Jillian has been involved in the maritime industry all her working life. Born in Oakville, Ontario, she joined the Canadian Coast Guard straight from high school, graduating as a navigation officer.

Her experience afloat included icebreaking, search and rescue and buoy tending. After coming ashore she worked in the rescue coordination centre (RCC) Halifax, the vessel traffic services centre Halifax and Saint John, New Brunswick. Ten years teaching at the Canadian Coast Guard College (CCGC) followed, covering vessel traffic services, maritime communications, and simulators. This included a bridge simulator; a BRM simulation; a VTS simulator; maritime radio communications (shore station radio); and global maritime distress and safety system (GMDSS).

She has worked with IALA in the development of VTS training and assisted in the design of the CCGC VTS simulator. She provided train the trainer courses at the CCGC for Canadian and foreign students and provided lectures for Norcontrol simulator user conferences.

She holds a Diploma of Nautical Science (Navigation); a Bachelor of Education (adult education) Universite de Moncton; a Master of Education (curriculum development) University of Toronto (Ontario Institute for Secondary Education) and is currently a PhD student at the University of Wollongong.

In 2002 she moved to work full time with IALA as technical coordination manager then in 2006 moved to AMSA to take on role of Manager, Vessel Tracking. She is currently the Manager, Vessel Traffic and Pilotage Services in the Maritime Standards Division of AMSA.

Chapter 5

The Harbour Master and pilotage relationships

By **John Dickinson** FNI

The relationship between the Harbour Master and the pilot in a particular port these days can be an unusual one, both professionally and legally. Much depends on the national legislation governing pilotage and safe navigation in that area and the amount of authority vested in the Harbour Masters or the entities that employ them.

Pilotage in most large commercial ports in the world can often be compulsory and in many cases the Harbour Master may be a senior pilot who has moved through the company system to management. In the case of many ports this position can be within the senior management team and this is where the relationship between the Harbour Master and pilot can come under different pressures, related to both operational issues and matters of remuneration.

In ports where the relationship is possibly not so formal, these pressures can be lower especially where Harbour Masters remain as working pilots as well as undertaking their statutory duties as Harbour Masters.

One widely used port authority operational model includes the statutory powers to regulate shipping and therefore control much of the commercial on-water activity within the harbour and the pilotage district. This model is often seen especially within the old Commonwealth countries. However times have moved on and there are now many different regulatory systems administering pilotage. For example pilotage may be regulated by the national maritime administration and the Harbour Master may work for an organisation that does not employ the pilots. However, the Harbour Master may still have statutory powers to regulate shipping and the authority to examine pilots and masters who apply and qualify for a Pilotage Exemption Certificate.

Such operational systems can potentially lead to conflict between pilots and Harbour Masters, unless the Harbour Masters have a good relationship with the pilots and the entity supplying their services. In the UK and elsewhere, pilots have viewed this type of regime as in some way removing from them a responsibility that was gained by hard work and study. The responsibility was then given to people who have not undergone the same training or who are familiar with the marine area. Some maritime administrations deem pilotage to be mainly a commercial enterprise despite the pronouncements of the IMO and other agencies which have long declared that pilotage is a service to society and to the port community. There are cases where more than one pilotage provider offers its service competitively in the same pilotage district. This can lead to further and difficult relationships as then Harbour Masters may be placed between the providers and yet need to be seen to be neutral and fair in their decisions at all times.

The Harbour Master and compulsory pilotage

As mentioned before, in most large commercial ports worldwide pilotage is compulsory; the sizes of the ships that fall into the compulsory category are set by the authority governing the pilotage waters. In some cases this will be governed by the local navigation and safety byelaws and the Harbour Master may ideally consult with the pilotage provider on this and any subsequent reviews. In some countries this requirement is enshrined within the national legislation. If the Harbour Master and the pilots are employed by the same employer this may be easier but industry and port users should ideally also be consulted in any changes to pilotage considered to the navigation and safety byelaws.

The Harbour Master and pilot training

Whether Harbour Masters are employed by the same entity as the pilots or by another authority, they may have a large contribution to make to pilot training. As the persons responsible for navigation and safety within their waters they have a valid interest in who is in control of vessels and thus the training of pilots serving a port.

The IMO adopted resolution A960 in 2003 Recommendations on Training and Certification and on Operational Procedures for Maritime Pilots other than Deep-Sea Pilots which defines elements of pilot operations. This includes matters to deal with the competent pilotage authority; the pilot's licence or certificate; medical fitness requirements; training; continued proficiency; a model syllabus for the pilotage exam and guidance on operational standards for a pilotage service.

Many well established pilotage areas had their own training regime which in the main followed the ideals of this resolution. Pilots generally see the benefit of medical standards and refresher simulator training as part of a structured CPD – continuing professional development – and authorisation or licence revalidation programmes. Many pilotage providers have made this a policy for some time but worldwide pilotage providers are a disparate group (as are Harbour Masters) and CPD is a new concept to many.

The Harbour Master, pilots and on water safety

One of the main responsibilities of Harbour Masters is in the role of safety on the water. One of the main weapons available to achieve this is harbour on water safety regulations, directions and byelaws. If these are properly drafted, they can be a help in the many aspects of Harbour Master's responsibilities in regard to water safety. Water safety covers many aspects of harbour, conservancy; competing interests such as recreational, commercial, pollution response and, in some areas, large public events. In ports where a pilotage service exists, the Harbour Master and pilots may find it is essential to work together to best ensure that safety on the water is not compromised in any way due to these disparate and sometimes conflicting activities. Pilots are essential for many aspects of on water safety. To ensure that commercial and recreational interests on the water are harmonised and at all times safe, they must be aware of and acknowledge the appropriate powers granted to the Harbour Master in this regard.

The Harbour Master and pilotage legislation

This is a very difficult subject on which to be informative; the legislation governing pilotage worldwide is so varied and different. However, with very few exceptions, the Master still has the overall command of the vessel. In some nations Masters will take advice from the pilot and in others (such as the UK) the pilot will be empowered by legislation to take charge of the conduct of the navigation of the ship (without compromising Masters' overall command of their ships). The requirement for berth to berth passage plans, good communication facilities and navigational technology that could have only been dreamed of in the recent past, have given Masters extra tasks. There are many ship's Masters who, after a very difficult and tiring passage to the pilot station, must greet the pilot on the bridge with a quiet sigh of relief. Yet in reality these Masters may not be aware of the actual status of pilots and their role on the bridge of the ship.

The Harbour Master, pilots and pollution incidents

In general, the public and those who work in a port area have an ever increasing awareness of all activities that are undertaken on the water, especially where pollution is concerned. There is also increasing awareness behalf of the public of the responsibilities of those who administer a port's regulations and those who work on the water. As a consequence, the relationship between pilots and the Harbour Master may come under greater scrutiny, not only where an incident incurring loss of life, personal injury or significant material damage occurs but also where pollution of even a minor nature happens. For example, a member of the public may find an oiled bird or their dog may get oil on its paws whilst walking on the beach. They then involve the media and it will not be too long before environmental groups are looking for someone to blame, especially someone in authority.

In any pollution incident the Harbour Master and pilots become a very important part of the response. Pilots are vital because of their detailed knowledge of the area, the weather and tides which can be invaluable when planning the response and determining the fate and movement of any spilled pollutant. Harbour Masters may wear two hats in any pollution response. They may be the person in charge of the response. On the other hand, they may also have the ultimate authority on the water to decide where to move ships or whether to close certain parts of the harbour, can ask for no-fly zones or other exclusion zones when decisions about public safety and good are involved.

Harbour Masters, pilots and the media

If there is an incident on the harbour to deal with there is likely to be much media interest, especially where pollution or other significant harm is involved. Harbour Masters and pilots must have a strategic policy which they both agree to in regard to any media requests for interviews, comments etc. Whether Harbour Masters and pilots work for the same organisation or not, their employers will undoubtedly have a media plan and if the company or local authority council is large enough it will have a media spokesman or team.

It must be remembered however that in the event of any accident or pollution incident the media will want something quickly, preferably an interview from a person of authority in relation to the incident. Therefore the Harbour Master and Pilots must have an agreed policy on how to respond to any requests from the media. If their employer has instructions on these matters then that may alleviate any concerns but especially in regard to Harbour Masters who may have the authority to comment to the press. In this case they must be circumspect in all media matters and preferably have received media training.

A note on geographical areas of responsibilities

The Harbour Master's area of responsibility may simply be a defined port; a safe area which includes the cargo berths, marinas and the pilotage areas and limits. There are ports at which these areas of responsibility may vary widely. A harbour may consist in an extreme form to take in all the territorial waters (12 nautical miles) from the nation's shoreline and may include all inland waters such as lakes and rivers. This broad scope of area definition places a greater responsibility on Harbour Masters. Such significant areas of responsibility potentially increase the scope for conflict between recreational and commercial traffic requirements. Under these circumstances Harbour Masters and pilots must liaise closely on any matters that could produce such conflict. It is also very relevant to all concerned that the intersts of the local fishing community need to be recognised. The best fishing grounds often appear to be in port approaches and pilotage areas where space may be limited!

This short chapter is a glance at the complex relationship that can exist between Harbour Masters and port pilots. Time, attitudes and legislation have changed considerably in the past two decades. Public expectations are different, especially with the increased access to and use of water and the competing interests.

John Dickinson FNI
Director @ IMO
The Nautical Institute

ABOUT THE AUTHOR

John started his career in the maritime industry with pre-sea training at Warsash Maritime Academy in the UK, followed by an apprenticeship with Furness Withy. He then served as third and second officer on various cargo, passenger and refrigerated ships both in New Zealand and the UK, with companies as diverse as Shaw Savill, the Union Steamship Co of New Zealand, Fred Olsen and Sea Containers. On gaining his Master FG (Class 1) he worked on the Boeing Jetfoil service from London to Ostend, Belgium. He then worked in the offshore sector in the Middle East as Master on supply ships, on a purpose built oil well test/flare ship, on pipe laying barges and construction barges and latterly as Master Offshore Installation Manager on drill ships off the coast of the UK.

On returning to New Zealand he worked as a ship planner with ACT, as Deputy Harbour Master in Wellington, then Harbour Master in the Port of Tauranga, moving to Maritime New Zealand, the maritime administration) as Harbourmaster for the Port of Taharoa. He was also the principal nautical examiner and manager licensing, responsible for all the maritime licensing in New Zealand.

image: Port of Hamburg

Chapter 6

The Harbour Master and tug operations

By **John Lee-Richards**

The role of Harbour Masters in ensuring safe commercial port operations is arguably one of the most important responsibilities of the position. Safe port operations have a direct bearing on the safety of life in the areas under the control of Harbour Masters, as well as protection of the nearby marine environment, and of course, the commercial success of ports.

Apart from overseeing and regulating pilotage and the management of the ports hydrography, the next most essential element is the safe handling of ships entering, berthing, and departing the port. A key contributing safety factor in these operations is the proper and effective use of the port's tugs.

The operation of navigating a ship safely from the pilotage boarding area to her berth is under the management of the harbour pilot. The pilot has the conduct of the ship; the Master is in command and can take over the navigation of the ship from the pilot if the situation requires it. Pilots will know the capabilities of the tugs at their disposal, the capabilities of the individual Tug Masters on the tugs, and how and where they have to manoeuvre ships to safely berth them.

Most well run ports have protocols relating to the safe operations of tugs. These may cover, but are not limited to, instructions on where tugs will meet ships; what speed ships should move through the water when 'picking up'; if tugs should be made fast to ships on a tow line; what length lines will be and many other important operational factors.

In recent times many ports around the world have developed 'succession' programmes which provide for the younger prospective harbour pilot, fresh from a career at sea, to start their port career as a Tug Master before graduating to be a harbour pilot. Pilots who have had the experience of being a Tug Master in a port, where they are later employed as a pilot, generally have a very good understanding of what a particular type of tug can and cannot do safely. Their expectations are moderated and enhanced by their former experiences. This tends to make for a very much safer operational environment for all concerned. The process ensures safer tug operations and introduces beginner pilots to shiphandling methods on a smaller scale.

As ships have become larger, and existing ports are restricted in their ability to expand, the operation of berthing a vessel safely has become much more complex. Large vessels now often require 'parking' in confined spaces. As a result, ports have been required to expand the numbers in their tug fleets and increase the capacity of their individual tugs, in terms of bollard pull.

There are a number of issues that should be considered by the Harbour Master in order to ensure safe tug operations, and these are set out here.

Rendezvous points for tugs meeting ships inbound

When considering berth layout and geography every port is different. Some ports are completely manmade with a solid breakwater surrounding a row of wharves, with the entrance to the port set at an angle so that minimal sea swell disturbs the tranquillity and safety of the port. Some are located up a natural river, and others might be located in a large natural harbour.

Whatever the port layout, much consideration goes into the decision about where the tugs will standby ready to meet the ship and become part of the berthing operation.

Escort tugs

There are really two distinct types of tug operations which occur close to a port that we need to consider, and that is escort tugs and harbour berthing tugs. It's not this author's intent to go into the role of escort tugs and how they operate, and which tugs are best for this type of operation. That subject is covered very adequately in another publication from The Nautical Institute, *Tug Use in Port*, by Captain Henk Hensen.

Escort duties are commonly required for two types of incidents. If vessels suffer engine or steering gear failure and need to travel in restricted areas, they may need breaking and steering assistance. Or, escorts will be needed when the passage of a ship in a restricted area is threatened by other ships, or if the first ship is off course and may threaten shoal ground.

In the case of escort tugs, rendezvous is made at the beginning of a planned long passage, often according to the dictates of legal statute or local regulation. The tugs are usually large and capable of stopping or steering a large loaded vessel efficiently. Escorts are normally undertaken at a relatively high speed (up to 12 knots). The escort area is sometimes outside of the Harbour Master's control; it is more likely to be under the control of a national authority.

Accordingly, pick up points for escort tugs are usually in an area which has a low navigational risk profile, and at the end or beginning of a sea voyage

Harbour berthing tugs

When the Harbour Master is considering a safe rendezvous point the following needs to be considered:

- Where will the ship need assistance with steering, positioning or stopping from an assisting tug as she approaches the port?
- What type of tugs does the port operate? Are they conventionally propelled tugs which will be required to lash up alongside, or will they be required to pick up a bow line or stern line while running in line with the ship to be assisted?
- What speed is safe and comfortable for a tug to approach a ship to put up a line?
- What swell and sea conditions are normally present at the port in the proposed pick up area?
- How close to the beginning of the berthing operation is the pickup point?

Time must be allowed for the tug to get into position, for the tug crew to put up a line or lines and secure the tug ready to assist. Tug passage time to the rendezvous point should be as short as possible to save fuel and labour costs for the tug and ensure the entering vessel does not have to slow down early and unnecessarily.

Turning to the releasing of tugs on departure, this is normally done by the ships' pilots when they are sure of the following:

- Ships have reached a point in the port approaches where speed has been increased safely and pilots are satisfied they have complete control over steerage, and ships will not be affected by wind, currents or shallow water
- There are no other areas in the transit ahead where tug assistance will be required again
- There is no danger of a ship/ship interaction occurring

This is not an exhaustive list of conditions which may compel a pilot to retain tug services but it does indicate the types of issues that need to be considered.

Safe tug handling procedures

As previously mentioned, the paramount objective of the regulator in any port environment is safety. Accordingly, monitoring of the working environment for dangerous practices is a priority for the Harbour Master. One of the areas of high risk in this regard is the day to day operations of the port's tugs, and central to this are the tug handling procedures adopted for the port.

Often, tug handling procedures have developed in a port by way of traditional processes over many years of operations. Mostly these procedures are found to be very sound, but often they may require some formalising for operational continuity and for legal reasons.

The Harbour Master in every port should have in place formal safe operating procedures for Tug Masters to follow, acknowledge and sign off. The procedures should be in the form of a manual that is readily available on each tug. These need to be controlled copies with updates made when required, for instance, as a result of an incident or the introduction of a new type of operation such as that following a new berth construction.

Often, these types of procedures are acknowledged initially, and then promptly forgotten. The Harbour Master's role, then, is to make sure that the procedures are current and that Tug Masters abide by them. This can be achieved by way of an annual audit process or a series of random checks by the Harbour Master's staff. The subject of safe tug handling procedures is covered in Tug Master training manuals, which form part of the operational management documentation in a port.

Safe tug handling procedures are important for a number of reasons, including: safety of the tug crew; safety of the crew on the ship being assisted; the safe navigation of the ship; the safe navigation of other ships in port and the protection of port facilities and the environment.

Tug orders

Tug commands around the world are many and varied and quite often become a point of contention and safety within a port, especially where a port has a large tug fleet, a large number of Tug Masters, either fully operational or in training, and a large team of pilots. There is generally much room for misunderstandings and the consequential safety risk. Traditionally, there has always been the 'personal touch' from pilots and Tug Masters alike which clearly endorses the individualism of ex-seafarers.

Some years ago, the Port of Los Angeles and the Port of Long Beach recognised this risk and a senior pilot operating in the port at the time, Captain Vic Schisler, devised a standard set of tug commands, in consultation with others in the industry. All operators, pilots and Tug Masters were urged to use the standard tug commands when engaged in shipping operations together. This protocol worked well and it was generally felt that safety was enhanced as a consequence. Obviously, standardised tug commands are best developed to suit the local port conditions and the personnel that operate there.

In reference to standardised tug commands, it is appropriate to recognise that some commands given by a pilot to the Tug Master can often cause confusion. Some time ago in an Australian port a particular pilot always asked the Tug Master to head for the church spire as he ran ahead of a large ship, on a line, up a river port. The problem with this order is that there were a number of church spires on the banks of this large river. The order was always answered with: "Would that be the Catholic church, or the Anglican church today Pilot?"

The purpose of standardised tug commands and the elimination of personalised commands are very necessary for the safety of shipping operations. For the aspirant Harbour Master, this is an operational risk that needs to be recognised, addressed and monitored. If formal risk assessments are a protocol of your port, tug commands should be an element of that risk assessment.

Tug boat training simulators

One of the key innovations in Tug Master training in recent years is the extension of ship manoeuvring simulators into the world of tug operations. Simulators are now available in various locations around the world for trainee Tug Masters to either learn the basic controls of the various types of tugs now operational, or the positioning of the tug boat into a desired position around a vessel, particularly while underway.

Simulators are also invaluable in familiarisation training for pilots and Tug Masters to help them understand each other's part of the ship berthing operation. These simulators are either owned by the tug companies themselves or public training institutions. Often, the bridge simulator is attached to a nautical college or training school and is therefore used as part of the training curriculum as candidates proceed through their qualifying courses. Some organisations involved in simulator training claim that simulators will reduce the training time of a new Tug Master by up to six months.

Simulators are often designed so that they can be quickly changed to provide the type of controls required for a particular type of tug propulsion system. For example, it may be a Voith Schneider tug simulation required on one day, followed by an ASD simulator the next day, or a conventional tug the day after. As previously mentioned, private tug companies often own simulators and because they operate a variety of different types of tugs require the ability to change the type of tug training available.

Simulators can be useful when training a Tug Master to assist with the range of different ship displacements. This is an important issue given the varying effects a tug will have on heavy vessels such as super tankers. While this issue is predominantly a pilotage issue, the Tug Master will be working alongside the pilot to provide an effective response.

An advantage of the simulator is that a particular manoeuvre can be carried out, the simulation can be paused at any point, and the manoeuvre can be discussed between the instruction and the student, before the simulation resumes. The writer's experience with simulators, particularly in the Voith Schneider mode, is that they are now provide a very close simulation to the real experience, but they should be used in parallel with the real on water experience to complete the proper training of Tug Masters. There are many tug operations that cannot be effectively simulated, such as the decision of the appropriate length of tow line to use. This is usually an element learned by experience on the water. However, if the opportunities exist for a trainee Tug Master to experience a tug simulator then this opportunity should be taken up.

The subject of training simulators is a very complex issue and there are publications available which cover the issue in depth.

Simulators are also frequently used to model particular ports. Then individual instances of the tug power needed under certain circumstances can be applied. It takes skill to determine the tug power required to safely handle a particular ship in a particular port, under different environmental conditions.

Conclusion

The broad subjects covered in this chapter are likely to be the most important issues that aspirant Harbour Masters should be aware of with regard to safe and efficient tug operations in the port. They will need to advise on, and monitor, safe tug operations in their port. Only then can they ensure safe port operations to protect the safety of life in the areas under their control, protection of the marine environment and continuity of commercial port operations.

John Lee-Richards

Retired Harbour Master and maritime consultant

ABOUT THE AUTHOR

John started his maritime career at 17 yrs old when he joined the Union Steam Ship Company of New Zealand Ltd as an apprenticed cadet in 1966. After qualifying with a second Mate's Certificate he joined Shell Tankers (UK) Ltd and then finished his time at sea with the Coastal Tankers Ltd in New Zealand. Coming ashore with a Foreign Going Master's Certificate he joined the Northland Harbour Board in New Zealand, operating conventional and Voith Water tractor tugs for eight years. During this time he assisted Voith with the training of Tug Masters in various locations around the world, a role he enjoys on a part-time basis to the present day. After three years as port Marketing Manager and Stevedoring Manager in Northland, John moved on to become Deputy Harbour Master in Northland. This was followed by a period as General Manager of New Zealand's Oil Spill Response Unit, based in Auckland, within what was then known as the Maritime Safety Authority of New Zealand. He then spent the last seven years of his formal working life as Harbour Master, Auckland, retiring from that role in 2011. John now spends his time on maritime consultancy projects and sailing.

Chapter 7

The Harbour Master and the mooring process

By Captain Ing **Ben van Scherpenzeel**

Good mooring processes are vital for ports and terminals. A ship breaking loose from its moorings is a big danger to other vessels and to the port infrastructure, which may not always be completely covered by insurance. A drifting vessel has a severe impact on cargo operations in the port and may even cause serious damage to cranes, cargo manifolds and fenders and injuries to staff ashore and afloat.

Good mooring processes lead to fewer accidents. Most personal injuries on board vessels are related to the failure of ropes under tension. Good mooring processes can contribute to greener operations. Reductions in greenhouse gas emissions can be made ships are brought quickly and safely alongside, enabling tugs to turnoff power plants and additional auxiliary engines much sooner than would otherwise be the case – surely a powerful incentive.

Thus a good mooring process is safe and efficient. But over the last few decades, vessels have become bigger and more complex, while the crew complement onboard has reduced. And not all crews are particularly well trained in mooring operations. Making a mooring process safer and more efficient at the same time might appear to be difficult to accomplish, but it is not impossible. So what can we do as Harbour Masters to improve the mooring process? It all starts with understanding.

First we need to understand all the components of a mooring system which consists of three elements:

The mooring winch onboard

The mooring winch has a brake that keeps the line under tension. The brake has a maximum load, called the maximum holding capacity (MHC). When this load is exceeded, the winch will render. But the MHC can change due to wear and tear and should be regularly tested. On many tankers this is already best practice.

The mooring line

The mooring line has a minimum breaking load (MBL). This MBL is recorded on the line's certificate, provided by manufacturers when ropes are delivered to the vessel. But the MBL can be reduced significantly over time due to wear and tear.

The mooring bollard or quick release hook ashore

The mooring bollard or quick release hook has a safe working load (SWL) at a certain maximum vertical angle, for example, 45°.

There is no international regulation for the relationship between these three components. But common sense dictates that the bollard ashore should be the strongest component. The mooring winch brake should always be the weakest link; it should give before the mooring line breaks. If the brake doesn't give, the mooring line will break first, which presents a big danger to all personnel in the vicinity of the mooring station.

Understanding what constitutes a good mooring plan is essential. It should take into account:

The length of the mooring lines between the fairlead and the bollard or hook. These should be a minimum of 35 metres and a maximum of 50 metres. This is to ensure that mooring lines have sufficient elasticity.

Length of mooring lines in the same service, for example all the breast lines, should be of the same length, elasticity and tension. This is to ensure that mooring lines work together. If lengths, elasticity or tensions are different from each other, the mooring lines will not work together.

Horizontal distance between fairlead and the bollard should be about twice the height difference, leading to a vertical angle of about 30°. This is to ensure that the horizontal component is sufficient to keep the vessel alongside. Larger vertical angles lead to less efficient mooring arrangements.

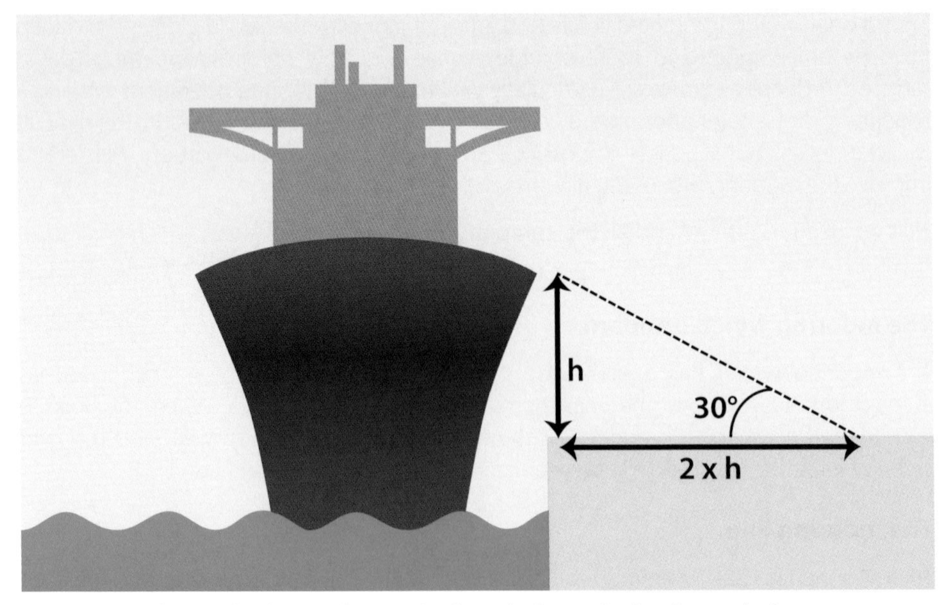

7.1 Mooring lines: the lower the vertical angle from the horizontal, the more efficient the mooring lines works

Spring lines or springs should be positioned parallel to the longitudinal centre line of the vessel.

Breast lines should be positioned at right angles to the longitudinal centre line of the vessel. Sometimes it's impossible to meet both the ideal horizontal and vertical angles of the lines due to the location of the bollards in relation to the ship's fairleads, especially at container and dry bulk terminals. In this case, first concentrate on meeting the minimum vertical angles, and then on the lead angles.

Understanding the mooring components and the mooring plan is essential for a good mooring process. For this, information is needed. Masters, pilots and linemen should be provided with mooring information before the vessel enters the port.

- Masters need information because they are ultimately responsible for the mooring process
- Pilots because they advise Masters
- Linemen because they assist in bringing vessel mooring lines ashore

If all parties have the same mooring plan, it negates the need for discussions and speeds up the mooring process.

Masters, pilots and linemen can be informed in three ways:

Information from terminal operators – Includes position and safe working load of bollards and hooks and the position of the vessel. Based on this information Masters can make mooring plans, possibly assisted by pilots, and then they can verbally inform linemen of the plan.

The terminal operator plan option one – This is based on a previous call of the vessel. The terminal operator can file mooring plans based on vessels' IMO numbers. This system is in use on wet bulk terminals.

The terminal operator plan option two – The terminal operator sends a mooring plan based on earlier calls of a sister vessel or a vessel of similar dimensions.

Regardless which of the three options is used, mooring plans need to be made before arrival at the berth, so mooring lines can be prepared before coming alongside.

Once vessels are berthed, it is important to keep them alongside. Best practice to keep the vessel alongside includes:

- Constantly check that lines are never slack. Slack lines allow vessels to move along berths, causing powerful dynamic forces
- Winches for spring lines should be held on the brake, rather than on auto-tension, to avoid vessels 'walking along the quay'
- Winches for breast lines may be put on auto-tension, but when wind or current is picking up, it is good practice to switch over from auto-tension to brake mode

The heaving capacity of a mooring winch in self-tensioning mode may be only 20 tonnes, while the same winch can have a brake holding capacity of 60 tonnes, three times more. Company policy with some container operators is to switch over at Force 6. Some terminals insist that auto-tension is never used.

If the wind picks up even more, a vessel can deploy additional lines. But this only makes sense if they are put under the same tension as the other lines. Paying out lines which are not winch lines is possible. It is very difficult to make them fast on bollards and to give them the same tension as the other lines. Additional lines without the same tension can give a false sense of security.

If it is not possible to pay out additional lines with the same tension, the second option is to order tugs of sufficient combined power to overcome the excess wind force and keep the vessel alongside. But if a port is faced with a decreasing number of tugs this last option becomes less and less realistic. Another option is to pay out shore lines to the vessel, and tension them ashore by means of hydraulic cylinders.

If all these options are not possible or when the safe working load of the bollards ashore is not sufficient, the correct decision should be to cast off the berth and proceed to sea to quickly seek safety in open water.

In all cases it's good practise to announce a warning to all vessels via VHF and advise terminals and agents if a gale or storm is expected.

Harbour Masters can improve mooring processes. Of course, in practice there is often little information available on a vessel to judge if indeed the winch-brake is the weakest link of all the components. But Harbour Masters have to ensure that vessels have been moored safely to protect infrastructure and other vessels, even if little information is available on maximum holding capacity and minimum breaking loads.

The least Harbour Masters can do is:

- Provide mooring plans to Masters, pilots and linemen
- Promote the training of pilots and linemen
- Promote the training of terminal operators. This last might seem strange as in the past many terminal operators had a nautical background. In recent years, the trend is for fewer to come this route and additional training might be necessary
- Inspect mooring lines and winches while vessels are alongside, ensuring crews keeps all mooring lines tight, spring lines on brakes and breast lines on brakes when wind speeds increase.
- Stencil safe working loads on top of bollards and quick release hooks
- Ensure the port bye-laws reflect internationally accepted guidelines such as OCIMF's *The Mooring Equipment Guidelines* and The Nautical Institute's *Mooring and Anchoring Ships, Volumes 1* and *2*
- Promote the European Harbour Masters' Committee video The Missing Link, improving the mooring process. This shows the entire mooring process, from the manufacture of a mooring line to the vessel coming alongside, and from the basic rules for a mooring plan to safe working loads and maximum holding capacities

Design of new berths

When it comes to the design of new berths, Harbour Masters are the link between the vessel, maritime service providers and the terminal. They are often asked for advice about the location of, and access to, mooring facilities.

For many construction companies this might be the first time of working on a berth or jetty, so it is good practice for them to sit together with pilots and linemen and discuss the plan before construction starts. This is a golden opportunity to improve the mooring plan and develop safe working spaces for linemen, which is often overlooked. Consultation at this stage can help to prevent damage during the jetty's use, as mooring lines under tension that are caught behind obstacles such as railings or corners can cause damage or injury. If a crew continues to heave in the line, it could break. A sudden release of a straining rope can pose a serious hazard to both linemen ashore and crewmembers at mooring stations on board the vessel.

Position and number of bollards and hooks

For both the construction of wet bulk, dry bulk and container berths a good mooring plan starts with the position of bollards or hooks. For tanker berths such as oil jetties, OCIMF provides recommendations in its *Mooring Equipment Guidelines*. All best practices have been collected in this publication. But details such as access ladders, railings and working spaces around quick release hooks should still be discussed with linemen.

For dry bulk and container berths guidelines can be found in The Nautical Institute's publication *Mooring and Anchoring Ships*. In general, it is good practice to reduce the intermediate distance between bollards and to use double bollards, allowing the vessel more flexibility to choose the best bollard for optimal vertical and horizontal angles. If it is possible to locate bollards further from the edge of the quay, it would improve the vertical angle, especially of the head lines, as their vertical distance to the quay is greater than those of the stern lines.

Safe working load of bollards and hooks

For tanker berths refer to the *Mooring Equipment Guidelines*. In general, hooks should be as strong as the minimum breaking load of the strongest mooring line anticipated with one line per hook.

For dry bulk and container berths there is no international rule for the relation between mooring lines and bollards. Common sense dictates that the bollard should at least be stronger than the weakest component of the entire mooring system, which is the brake on the winch. Given the fact that the setting of these brakes is not totally reliable, the safest approach is to stick to the OCIMF recommendation: safe working loads should be as strong as the minimum breaking load of the strongest line anticipated. If it is the intention to put more lines on one bollard, the safe working load should be increased accordingly. Bear in mind that many new container vessels have mooring lines with an MBL of 130 tonnes.

Bollards and hooks; capstans or not?

Quick release hooks and capstans are much more expensive than bollards, both in their initial cost as well as in maintenance. Some circumstances dictate the use of quick release hooks and capstans. The main issue is the weight of the mooring lines to be handled this is dictated by three issues:

Mooring line lengths: those on mooring dolphins for tanker berths can be substantially longer compared with those at container berths

Mooring line materials: tankers often use wires rather than synthetic lines, the weights of which differ widely

Mooring line positions: if mooring lines are in the water, the weight is much more, especially a wire line, when compared to a line which has to be manoeuvred over the quayside

In turn these three issues lead to the following choices of the type of berth needed.

7.2 Mooring line choices

Type of berth	Vessel size	Mooring arrangement	Comments
Tanker berths and oil jetties	Below 40,000dwt	Bollards with capstans	Mooring dolphins cannot be reached by winch vehicles
Tanker berths and oil jetties	Over 40,000dwt	Quick release hooks with capstans	Quick release hooks preferred for tanker berths as the line can be released in an emergency while it is still under tension
Dry bulk and container berths or quays	Below 40,000dwt	Bollards and no capstans	
Dry bulk and container berths or quays	Over 40,000dwt	Use only bollards and capstans if bollards cannot be reached by winch vehicles or are not available	If quick release hooks are chosen, they must be well maintained or they are prone to jamming

7.3 Working in front of the quick release hook

Safe working spaces for linemen

As mentioned before, a safe working space for linemen is often forgotten and attention should also be given to the maximum weight to be handled. The Netherlands Royal Boatmen Association, Eendracht, together with ergonomics experts and experts in the construction of berths and jetties, have together studied this issue.

Tanker berths

Quick release hooks with a safe working load of less than 75 tonnes: a minimum of 50cm next to and in front of the hook in an open position

Quick release hooks with a safe working load of more than 75 tonnes: a minimum of 50cm next to and 90cm in front of the hook in an open position

7.4 Work space is needed by the side of bollards to release lines

7.5 Lashing devises should have covering lids

Dry bulk and container berths

Minimum distance between centre line of the bollard and the edge of the quay: 50cm
Minimum space by the side of the bollards, parallel to the quay: 90cm
Minimum space behind the bollard for vessels smaller than 40,000-dwt: 120cm
Minimum space if bollards need to be accessible for winch vehicles: 3.5 meters
Minimum space if bollards are placed in pairs: 50cm between the two of them

As container cranes are getting larger and larger due to the increasing beam of container vessels, it is imperative that attention is paid to the minimum distance between the container crane and the bollard; this should be minimum of one metre. It must be appreciated that crane operators do not always realise that there is somebody working on the quay when they start driving. Lashing devices for cranes should not be located next to bollards. If they are, they should be covered by lids to prevent linemen stepping into the recess.

There is no doubt that for existing, and for the development of new berths, Harbour Masters play an important role in ensuring that the mooring process is safe and efficient, resulting in a safe and efficient port and their contribution is necessary.

image: Port of Los Angeles

Chapter 8

The Harbour Master and terminal and cargo operations

By **Alan Coghlan**

In practical terms, there is no rigid structure within which a Harbour Master is connected with either terminal or cargo operations. There are however, statutory obligations imposed on Harbour Masters which bring them into direct contact with both terminal operators and cargo operations.

- In some ports Harbour Masters may be port operations managers and have total managerial responsibility
- In other ports they may not even be managers and report to port operations managers
- Harbour Masters may work in ports which neither own nor operate any terminals
- Conversely Harbour Masters may work for port companies which own and operate all or some facilities within their port

So you can readily see that in some ports the practical connection is difficult to define whilst in others it may be more concrete.

There is however one undeniable fact – Harbour Masters are responsible for the time and manner that ships are taken into and out of ports. They are also responsible for the allocation of a suitable berth to every ship. Among the issues that inform the decision about time and manner of entry or departure is the type and quantity of cargo on board. This is particularly so in the case of dangerous or hazardous cargoes. It is also very important to be aware of the needs of receivers or terminal operators. These requirements will include the time that has been allocated to discharge or load and the rotation of ships required to come to their terminals.

When it comes to the allocation of a berth at a terminal, there may be mandatory separation distances required to be applied between ships either by national laws or local byelaws. Similarly Harbour Masters may have the duty to control the conditions of loading or unloading of hazardous cargoes in terms of the hours of work and dwell time in the port. So already it can be clearly seen that Harbour Masters need to interact with terminal operators and cargo operations.

Taking the case of a port which does not own any terminals or engage in cargo work, the question is how does regulation by the Harbour Master relate to the commercial well being of the private terminal operator? The commercial well being of a private terminal within a port generally increases the port company's own commercial return. The creation of conditions and infrastructure within which a private terminal can successfully operate is generally seen as a prime objective of a port company. Also important are the requirements of the terminal operator as they will have invested significant capital in the setting up of their venture within the port.

This exchange of requirements can best be achieved through a series of meetings. It must be realised that the Harbour Master may not even be party to those discussions, this is particularly so where the Harbour Master is not a member of the management team. If you are in such a situation then you must impress upon your company negotiation team the importance of your requirements as Harbour Master and the mandatory legal requirements that may be imposed either through national or local legislation. Your requirements will generally hinge around the issues of legislative controls, navigational safety, permitted draughts at terminals and hazardous cargoes.

Containerised marine transport has for many years dominated international trade. This has added to the difficulties of the Harbour Master for two principal reasons – the multiplicity of different, and possibly hazardous cargoes that may be on any one container ship, and the tremendous time pressure that is part and parcel of container trade.

The importance of cargo information

It is vital that the Harbour Master's Department be made aware of any and all hazardous cargoes stowed on board any ship entering the port. Thankfully within Europe this is now very efficiently handled through the National Single Window through which all information about an arriving and departing ship is passed to all relevant agencies – including Harbour Masters. This pre-arrival/departure information allows Harbour Masters to efficiently plan ships' arrivals and departures from ports. It also enables them to impose any additional requirements they may consider necessary, due to the risks involved as a direct result of the nature of the cargo on board.

Hazardous cargoes are not limited to containerised traffic as bulk carriers quite often have hazardous or sensitive cargoes in large quantities on board. Some fertilisers, such as ammonium nitrate, are considered high risk cargoes. In some jurisdictions the handling of this cargo is subject to government control. This control dictates the hours of work and does not allow loaded trucks to remain in the port under any circumstances.

Similarly, bulk liquid cargoes such as hydrocarbons and chemicals are considered hazardous or high risk and may require a Harbour Master under legislation, to impose restrictions on the hours of work in the interest of safety, as well as control of naked flames or lights.

Commercial pressures

As Harbour Master you will be subject to pressure from many directions. The most common of these that you can expect is the commercial pressure exerted by terminal operators because of their need to carry out efficient and cost effective operations. This pressure will include the need to maximise berth occupancy at their terminals. They only make money while a ship is alongside and working. Often in the past this has led to such practices as terminal operators asking ships' crews to let go some deck cargo lashings before reaching the berth. Do you as Harbour Master consider this a safe practice within the port? In periods of very bad weather who makes the decision to cease container operations at a terminal? If it is not the Harbour Master there must be a very clear line of responsibility as to who it is that will make such a decision at a container terminal and more importantly the Harbour Master must be informed when such a decision is made as this will have immediate effect on ship movements which will involve extra planning.

You may be asked to reduce, or dispense with mandatory separation between some vessels in order to accommodate an extra ship alongside. In ports with a strong tidal regime you may well be pressured to berth a vessel at the totally wrong state of the tide. My only advice in all of these circumstances is to ensure that all the parties realise what your function is and your duties under legislation be it, regional, national and local. This can only be achieved through dialogue and a clear explanation of why these types of regulations are necessary.

Another common pressure is the allocation of berths which should be to a strict order of arrival. This should apply particularly where a general user facility is available for use by various agencies and stevedoring companies. In such these cases, each stevedoring company will be anxious to have the vessels they are contracted to serviced as quickly as possible. There will inevitable, but understandable, arguments over which ship arrived first. It is therefore important that as Harbour Master you have clear published rules as to what constitutes an arrived vessel and a definitive method of establishing the order of arrival. May I suggest the use of VTS to solve this problem? Even in ports which do not have the volume of business to support VTS, recordable radar or AIS, which gives historical output, should monitor the point at which you declare ships must have passed to be an arrived ship.

In general user facilities there will be berths which can be used as bulk dry and bulk liquid berths. If you offer such services at a single berth you may be faced with the problem of a tanker arriving to discharge at a berth which is occupied by a discharging bulk carrier. The ship on the berth has priority. However, there may be an opportunity, perhaps over a weekend when bulk discharge has ceased, to enable the tanker to discharge. In such cases the Harbour Master has the authority to order the bulk carrier off the berth, bring in the tanker to complete discharge and have the bulk carrier back on the berth for resumption of work on a Monday morning. This will have implications for the bulk carrier, in terms of the cost of assistance such as pilotage, tugs and linesmen, but the port will have served an extra ship without delaying the vessel originally on the berth. It is not uncommon, where a port can service a second vessel in such circumstances, to make a contribution to the additional cost imposed on the first vessel that has to vacate the berth. This is a matter of internal port commercial policy.

This will not be an issue where the problem occurs at a private facility. Under those circumstances it is the facility operator which decides the rotation of ships at its facility, and it your duty to work to that preference.

Other factors

The actions of a Harbour Master can sometimes be regarded as unhelpful by stevedores and agents. This is particularly the case where, due to wind conditions, you may decide to berth a ship with a very dusty cargo in a position that will not contaminate other cargoes being worked nearby. One common example is coal being discharged adjacent to terminals handling animal feeds. You may have to instruct the ship discharging animal feed to shift to another berth and bring the vessel with coal to the original berth. This will be seen as a delay to the animal feed vessel, but you have accommodated the second vessel, thereby making the facility available to as many vessels as possible, which is your prime responsibility.

Most Harbour Masters also have regulatory responsibility for the setting down of cargoes on quays or jetties prior to loading. This is an integral part of port operations, but the Harbour Master's function is to ensure optimum use of the quays for as many customers as possible. Problems arise where cargo set down interferes with the loading or discharge of another vessel and, more importantly, interferes with the clear passage of responders in the event of an emergency on a ship alongside or elsewhere on the quay.

Moorings and the method chosen by the Harbour Master can lead to difficulties in cargo operations. This is very evident in the case of breast lines which sometimes must be deployed across the quay. The problem is evident but this action may well be very necessary for the safety of ships in periods of very high winds. There is, however a very interesting solution offered by the Dutch Boatmens' Association (Nederlandse Bootlieden Vereniging). This involves a pre-tensioned shore unit fixed to a mooring line. This was developed from their members' experiences at container terminals at which the deployment of breast lines precluded any cargo operations.

Environmental issues arising from cargo operations are sometimes the responsibility of the Harbour Master. Such problems can be significant where a facility is located in or close to a residential area. Problems can arise through dust migration or though noise. Both cause considerable problems for nearby residents. In such cases it is advisable to have agreed wind directions and parameters agreed with stevedores. This is not a great problem where the wind direction is off shore or away from residential areas. There are even instances when the wind is onshore but, depending on conditions, there may be wind strengths within which you can allow terminals to continue to operate. Even so, it is normally the port, in the person of the Harbour Master, who will have to make the decision on the day. Publish your agreed parameters, make them widely known and stick to them. This will provide you with protection in the event of a dispute.

A relatively new problem is been the issue of odour from cargo operations. It is hard to say exactly how this should be tackled. Some ports, such as Esperance in Australia, have devoted considerable resources to the mitigation of this issue and a visit to its website may be of value to those Harbour Masters encountering such problems.

In the case of noise pollution, it is advisable to have a handheld decibel meter to enable you to verify definitively the level of noise generated by cargo operations, and establish whether or not these are above permissible levels. In cargo operations it is important to satisfy as far as possible the concerns of all stakeholders. It is even more important to show that you have a policy which enables you to take steps to mitigate the effects of operations where they lead to complaints from residents or other stakeholders.

Emergency planning

As Harbour Master you will have a pivotal role in emergency planning and response. This is particularly so if there is an emergency on a ship within the port. As part of the response to such an emergency you may have to disrupt cargo operations on adjacent ships or indeed have to order them to vacate their berths for the duration of the emergency. This will have a very direct knock-on effect on ship scheduling, more so in container facilities where time is vital. There are problems associated with all cargoes and common examples of those which might pose problems include the escape of gases from cargo, fires or excessive temperature in coal cargoes, grain fires and animal feed fires. In all such cases Harbour Masters will have to make decisions in response to the emergency that will have a direct effect on the working of other ships in the vicinity. Bear this in mind – it is better to be damned for doing something than for doing nothing.

Conclusion

Cargo operations are central to the life of a port. The Harbour Master has various regulatory duties which impact on these operations. Why is this so? The Harbour Master in most ports is a statutory officer whose functions are clearly defined in the interest of both the common good and that of the port. These duties clearly impact on the operation of discharging and loading of ships. It is also interesting to note that all qualified merchant marine personnel are the only people whose qualifications include a complete knowledge of the carriage and handling of cargoes carried in ships. We are also expected to make decisions in relation to the safety of ships' personnel and their property.

It is also true to say that the decisions we make do have effects on the operations conducted at quay and the facilities with ports. Generally it is accepted that our decisions are made in the best interest of all concerned, but occasionally your decisions will result in commercial disruption and inconvenience to cargo operators within the port.

Ports and their trades differ and there are as many solutions as there are problems, with each solution tailored to conditions in each port

In the case of hazardous cargoes, no Harbour Master can be expected to have a complete knowledge of each and every hazardous material. Every Harbour Office should have a copy of the IMO *Blue Book* either in hard copy or electronic format. This will at least allow you to consider how such cargoes should be handled. If you are in a port where there is a consistent trade in one or two types of hazardous material it is then very important that you become very familiar with all the issues surrounding such cargoes.

Chapter 9

The Harbour Master and port security

This chapter examines how ports, and Harbour Masters in particular, can deal with security. This issue rose to the top of the agenda when the ISPS Code was introduced in 2002, a year after the 9/11 attacks in the USA. First the landside of security is examined and then the threat from the waterside of a port.

Landside security

By **Alexander Surikov**

In the past, commercial port security was very much land-orientated and concerned with deterring theft, the passage of illegal immigrants and countering smuggling and contraband. Some smaller ports had no security measures of importance at all and the public was free to walk on the wharves. Security might have been tight at the warehouse but was not on the pier. Other, larger ports had their own police forces. Even they were not very often concerned with matters other than theft. In some other countries, all ports were considered military installations and, therefore, security came as second nature to their administrations.

Military installations apart, for the rest of the port world, and Harbour Masters in particular, wider security first began to be a major topic of concern when the ISPS Code was introduced. Globally, threat levels were raised to red alert and authorities at ports and airports were forced to scrutinise their security provision.

There is no doubt that Harbour Masters have a vital role in port security, even though the exact scope of their involvement may differ from country to country or even from port to port.

Control of access

The development of access control will depend on the size, location and capability of the port in supporting the security plan, but landside security measures could include:

- CCTV
- Barriers
- Port police
- Port identification cards
- Roving patrols

9.1 Control of access to landside areas can include patrols (image: Port of Primorsk)

Port boundaries

As Harbour Master you have some, if not all, of the responsibility for developing the port's security and access control plans. How far should your responsibility extend? This is a grey area in the ISPS Code which deals with the port/ship interface, but makes no reference to, or definition of, port boundaries. Therefore if Harbour Masters are not port security officers, they should have a close working relationship with them.

Port approaches

There is no doubt that the approaches to the port are more vulnerable today than in the past. Distances within ports and the limitations of surveillance equipment make it difficult to uncover threats to shipping in time to intercept the perpetrators. Two ways forward are possible for Harbour Masters. The first is to encourage good cooperation with state security forces which will be constantly monitoring all operations in the port approaches. If these forces receive information about proposed unlawful actions they will inform the Harbour Master and act according to pre-developed plans. The second way is to use the port's own security department or even to hire security companies. In this case the Harbour Master has to judge which company would be best qualified for the job. These security companies should work together with the Harbour Master to protect shipping routes on approaches to the port.

Most likely targets

It is widely thought that specialised vessels such as tankers and passenger vessels are most likely to attract attacks and indeed this is the case. However, we must take into account the terrorists' motives. These may be political demands, economical destruction or even groundless protest. Threats are real for any vessel in any port. Harbour Masters in all ports should be ready for such threats.

Port facility security officer

A port facility security officer is, according to the ISPS Code, the person responsible for the development, implementation, revision and maintenance of the port facility security plan and for liaison with the ship security officers and company security officers.

Who has the role of the port facility security officer? This will differ widely from country to country; it may be the Harbour Master, or a representative from either a stevedoring company or the national or local maritime administration. Some ports have several port facility security officers, depending on the number of facilities within their jurisdictions.

Under the ISPS Code port facility security officers, in addition to any other duties, are expected to:

- Maintain communication protocols for ships and port facilities
- Prevent unauthorised access to ships, port facilities and restricted areas within them
- Enforce prohibition of unauthorised weapons, incendiary devices or explosives onboard ships or in port facilities

The Code says port facility security officers must be given the powers to exercise these duties and responsibilities, including proper financial resources.

Control of ships in port

Under IMO regulations, all vessels of 500gt and over on international voyages must provide to the arrival port in advance of arrival a completed form detailing the security status of the vessel and previous ports of call. Harbour Masters and port security officers should scrutinise the information contained in these forms. They should verify that ships are in possession of valid International Ship Security Certificates or valid Interim certificates issued under the provisions of Part A of the ISPS Code.

If such a certificate is unavailable or invalid, there are escalating levels of measures that can be taken against the vessel:

- Inspection
- Delay
- Detention
- Restriction of operations, including movements within the port
- Expulsion of the ship from the port

Declaration of security

Declarations of security (DoS) may be required by port facilities under the ISPS Code when needed. These are useful for small ports which do not have a plan in place.

Training and exercises

Harbour Masters and port facility security officers have a major role to play to ensure ports meet their responsibilities for security training, drills and exercises. These offer an important opportunity to check how well the security system works. Any gaps or anomalies shown by these exercises will lead to revisions in security plans.

It is clear that since 2001, port security has risen to the top of the agenda in terms of importance – the IMO has seen to that. Security is as vital as safety and the protection of the environment. Harbour Masters have a vital role in the whole security setup and are crucial to the success of security procedures of any port.

Waterside security

By **Jaap Lems**

Terminals are now quite capable of providing security at the 'back door' – at the access to the quays landside – but are more vulnerable at the 'front door'. Additional 'eyes and ears' at the front door – the waterside – would benefit terminals and ports. Creating awareness is one of the basic cornerstones in this. Cooperation and awareness on the waterside of a port should be an additional 'layer' in anti-terrorism measures to complement the ISPS Code and help meet the requirements of the European Parliament's regulation 65/2005.

The European Harbour Masters' Committee has investigated the attitude of Harbour Masters to an enhanced security role for service providers in a port, such as boatmen, who could offer additional observation support. The case is that these people are frequently – and throughout working hours – operating in the port area.

Harbour Masters were in general positive about this suggestion, agreeing that waterside security is a concern and that people working at the 'front door' could have a role in security measures. European Harbour Masters feel that improved awareness and control were necessary and that waterside security must be improved. Boatmen could be important – becoming the 'eyes and ears' of a port because of their numbers and the nature of their activities which see them moving alongside quays at all times. Boatmen also know their ports, know the regularly visiting vessels, know the Harbour Masters and their organisation, know how to communicate with other parties and have the appropriate equipment at their disposal to this end, such as vessels and radio equipment.

Several European ports are discussing, or already have in place, voluntary participation from port service providers in their security networks and are considering how to use this expertise to improve the chances of foiling different types of attacks.

On the other hand, some Harbour Masters are reluctant to use boatmen, believing their value is limited because of the nature of their activities – they are often in a hurry to move from one ship to another. When mooring, they are alert to the need to prevent accidents rather than enhance security, it is argued. Other reservations centre on the role of Harbour Masters in different countries. They may not be responsible for waterside security and could put in place systems that conflict with those offered by professional security enterprises.

It would be wise to train personnel in security matters, including Harbour Masters' patrol vessel crews and port service providers, such as the boatmen. Training should be conducted, when possible, with police forces. This training should teach them to identify suspicious circumstances. If more people in the port are trained to be aware of unusual activity and to alert the Harbour Master's office or police, then security will be improved.

Cooperation with boatmen or other service providers will also be very useful in, for instance, conducting surveys on the waterside at sensitive berths – such as those used by cruise ships.

Harbour Masters must then be aware that they must have a mechanism for notifying all these 'additional' personnel of extra activities in the port – such as diving. If people are uninformed these activities will easily be misinterpreted as hostile. There has to be a proper organisation in the Harbour Master's office to process this information, including cross-checking details, before police or security forces are called.

Any possible conflict with the work of professional security agencies should be avoided. Whether using boatmen or other port workers in security roles, the same rules should apply to them as to security organisations. Vetting of personnel will be vital. It is important to train everyone in the use of the information they gather. We do not want to spread panic.

The three security levels that the ISPS Code defines can be taken as a starting point to organise things. For instance, staff need to be told exactly what their tasks are as 'eyes and ears'; to know whether collaboration is voluntary and to be given a definition of their responsibilities.

Security level 1

At this level, collaboration may be largely voluntary and may be seen as 'good citizenship'. A VTS system may be sufficient to cover the 'front door'. The prime role would be that of awareness assistance and the reporting of anything unusual. In training use should be made of the experiences of the airport officials and general police forces. All those who might be called upon to assist the port security officer and the Harbour Master will need to be trained in how to recognise possibly unusual activities on the waterfront. These might include:

- Unusual objects attached to a ship's hull
- Maintenance work on ships' berths (to be checked with the port authority)
- Preparations for diving activities
- Pleasure boats close to or at ships' berths

- Other unusual observations that point to observation of port activities or preparation for unusual activities

Security levels 2 and 3

At these higher levels of security another kind of support should be deployed. Harbour Masters may need to more strictly regulate shipping traffic to, from and within the port and harbour basins. But it may be difficult to achieve this as resources will be stretched and there may be a shortage of, for instance, patrol craft.

At these levels cooperation is not voluntary and would involve utilising the skills of boatmen, equipment and other personnel. Tasks could include surveying the waterside in front of those piers, berths or vessels considered vulnerable; for example those occupied by cruise ships with US nationals onboard. A prime role at levels 2 and 3 would thus be observational, supporting observations from Harbour Masters' patrol vessels.

At some point between levels 2 and 3 there may be the need for additional restrictions to navigation. These restrictions include the banning of fishery, recreational or high speed craft and a prohibition on vessels entering the harbour basin unless absolutely necessary.

A combined force of port and police vessels may monitor harbour approaches to ensure only vessels with a verified destination in the port enter the harbour basin. Appropriate action may be taken if this is not the case.

Implementation of this monitoring system will require increased efforts on behalf port security or police officials, especially if the port has a large trade from smaller craft such as inland barges. Monitoring their movements will require large resources from VTS operators who may need assistance to identify barges that do not respond to radio calls or other communication attempts. At this level of security the supervision of public areas will be intense.

At both levels 2 and 3 boatmen can support the Harbour Master with defined tasks such as:

- Observation and contacting unidentified smaller craft including barges
- Acting as a Harbour Master patrol vessel with a Harbour Master official on board
- General monitoring of port areas observing people, vessels or vehicles in suspicious places

All these are tasks that would normally be carried out by government officials. It goes without saying that only those who have been stringently vetted should carry out any of these extra duties.

Preparations

Once the port is under threat, everybody needs to know what their role should be; it is necessary to drill staff from all organisations so they work cooperatively. This means not only giving instructions, but also ensuring the different teams get to know each other.

Preparations may consist of:

- Working instructions, including communications procedures Awareness courses
- Joint training sessions, including awareness and observation
- Regular joint tests of procedures and equipment
- Regular drills and exercises for staff

In addition to these preparations an agreement is needed to ensure all parties know what to expect from one another and where the responsibilities lie.

Security under the waterline

Securing the port above the waterline is not that easy. However, underwater defence is even more complicated. That is why we, as Harbour Masters, would seek to use suitable underwater detection equipment, so officials can be warned in a timely manner if unauthorised persons or underwater craft are approaching or in the port area. Prototypes exist to show the tracks of divers or underwater craft on computer screens, but the cost of such equipment needs to be reasonable.

Alexander Surikov
Harbour Master
Port of Primorsk

Before moving to become Harbour Master of Primorsk Port in 2006, Alexander served with the Russian maritime authority in St Petersburg. He came ashore in 2005 after serving as an officer on merchant vessels, rising to the rank of Master. He attended the State Maritime Academy, St Petersburg before serving as a navigator on vessels. Since 2010 he has held the voluntary post of web administrator of the International Harbour Masters' Association site www.harbourmaster.org

Jaap Lems

ABOUT THE AUTHOR

Jaap served in the merchant marine and has held several posts since coming ashore. These have included: chief safety inspector of dock labour for the Dutch Ministry of Social Affairs; head of the nautical policy department at the Ministry of Public Works and Transport; project manager, ships wastes and infrastructure for the Port of Rotterdam Authority, Chief Harbour Master Rotterdam. For this last post he was also mandated to be the regional state Harbour Master and the regional port security authority for Rotterdam-Rijnmond. He has served as Chairman of EHMA (later EHMC) and vice-president of IHMA. On retirement he volunteered to become the IHMA's development officer, and became Chairman of the Dutch nautical training centre for and regional chairman of the Inland Barge Masters' Association.

image: Port of Los Angeles

Chapter 10

The Harbour Master and the environment

By **Geraldine Knatz**

Port and harbour managers must be committed to managing port operations and development projects in an environmentally responsible manner. Both the communities that surround the port and regulatory authorities will expect the port's administration to strive to minimise the impacts of its activities. These include those activities that may not be within the direct jurisdiction of the port, such as vessels, trucks, terminal operations and trains. The expectation is that the port will have implemented pollution prevention measures and have programmes that support the continuous improvement of the port and surrounding environs. The ability of the port to carry out its traditional functions can often depend on how well environmental matters and concerns are addressed. This chapter outlines the fundamental principles that port managers should consider when developing their environmental programmes or plans. It covers the information the port must collect in order to develop an environmental plan and concludes with a list of available global references that that provide useful tools or examples.

Successful ports typically have a comprehensive environmental plan or programme to ensure that all significant environmental issues are considered in its overall operations and development. Further, there is increasing pressure on ports to ensure operations are environmentally sustainable. In addition, new areas of environmental concerns are continually emerging, such as the need to reduce greenhouse gases, and these must be addressed continually.

Port environmental plans should be designed to evolve over time to address additional and new sources of environmental impacts, as well as deal with new and emerging environmental issues and concerns. Environmental programmes may best initially focus on activities under the direct control of the port, such as its owned and operated equipment, port funded construction projects and other port funded activities and operations. Once the port itself has demonstrated environmental leadership, it will facilitate the enhancement and growth of the port's environmental programmes to address the impacts of port users. This can include the activities of port users that may extend beyond the geographical boundary of the port.

What should a port's environmental plan include?

The appropriate environmental policies, plan, and programmes for any port need to address the specific circumstances of that individual port. A major urban port is going to need to focus on different environmental issues from those facing a port located within an ecologically significant estuary. Further, each port has its own unique operations and uses. These could include liquid bulk terminals, container cargoes, break bulk facilities, the fishing industry and canneries, shipyards, recreational facilities and so on. Each port also has its own unique governance structure, such as landlord ports, facility operators, combination ports and state owned operations. All of these aspects must be considered when developing an environmental plan.

The foundation of any plan is the development of a general environmental policy, which will be used to guide development and implementation of programmes over a period of time. The policy should be broad in nature and establish the overall environmental goal for the port. Based upon that policy, an environmental plan can be developed.

The environmental plan should include:

- Baseline conditions
- Various programmes and measures
- Priorities
- Implementation schedule
- Metrics for evaluating effectiveness and updating frequency and procedures

Community members are often suspicious of port collected scientific results. The public may make the assumption that the port has a vested interest in presenting only positive results. Therefore, inclusion of the regulatory agencies in the development of port environmental programmes can enhance the plan's credibility, especially for the general public. While regulators sometimes expect the port authorities to do more than they can, the inclusion of the regulatory staff and the general public in plan development improves the transparency of the process. Use the plan development as an opportunity to educate the regulators and the general public about port operations while building long term relationships.

Compiling an environmental plan for your port

Compiling a comprehensive plan for an individual port requires the knowledge of existing conditions and an assessment of the legal and regulatory framework with which the port must comply. These two elements form the basic foundation for the preparation of an environmental plan.

Baseline development

A study of existing environmental conditions in and near the port will establish a baseline which will be useful for measuring the progress of the port's environmental plan. Both the physical and the natural environment should be surveyed. For most ports, the relevant parameters of any plan would include:

- Air quality, including greenhouse gas emissions
- Water quality
- Waste generation and reduction
- Soil contamination
- Dredging and disposal operations
- Storm water run-off
- Natural resources including habitats and wildlife
- Energy conservation
- Noise
- Cultural resources such as historic, areas of cultural significance and archaeological
- Sustainability
- Human health
- Environmental justice, or the extent to which facilities with negative impacts influence, disproportionately affect, or are located by low income or minority populations

One issue that ports struggle with is defining the boundaries of their environmental baseline. Naturally, the environment within the port area is the primary focus of the port's environmental programmes. But for certain environmental issues, such as air emissions and greenhouse gases, it may be appropriate for the port's environmental plan to consider areas and activities outside the port complex itself. In such cases, the environmental baseline for those environmental aspects would need to address such extended areas. Relevant examples include trains leaving the port and blocking streets at crossings, such as intersections between roads and railways, or air and water pollution emissions that move beyond the boundaries of the port to influence the surrounding region.

A regulatory baseline should also be developed. All applicable local, regional, national, and international environmental regulations should be identified and listed. Regulations with future implementation dates should be included.

Development of environmental plan programmes, schedules, and metrics

The environmental baseline should be evaluated within the context of the environmental policy established by the port, the most significant environmental issues facing the port and current and pending environmental regulations. As a result of this analysis, the port will find that it may or may not be meeting regulatory requirements or that its activities contribute to the inability to meet a certain regulatory threshold for a larger geographical region. The results of this evaluation will be important in the prioritisation of environmental issues that require additional action by the port.

It should be noted that many ports have found that meeting the requirements imposed by regulatory authorities, while a key component of any environmental programme, is not enough. Today, meeting regulatory requirements is essential and ports should continue to look for continuous environmental improvements. A port that wants to position itself as an environmental leader may chose to do more than regulators require. A more proactive approach to develop additional environmental programmes and measures that go beyond regulatory authority or which address environmental areas not yet regulated can have significant benefits. Not all measures that go beyond regulatory authority will be cost-prohibitive. Look for opportunities that are unique to your particular operation or locality. It may take only one small operational measure that the port adopts that can set it down the path of environmental leadership.

Others will take considerable investment initially but can provide future cost savings. For example, even if your local government does not require the port to conform to any type of green building code or standards, there are significant benefits that can come from voluntarily implementing green building practices. Green building practices result in long-term operational cost savings through reduced usage of energy and potable water, and minimising waste and wastewater generation. They also provide a public relations opportunity for the port that could be helpful when dealing with local governments and communities. It is beneficial for port mangers to consider ways the port can be a leader in environmental initiatives, with the opportunity for recognition through positive publicity.

Environmental programmes and measures should be identified to tackle the most important environmental issues to be currently addressed. Further, the sources of impact associated with those environmental issues that will initially be focused upon should also be identified. As previously indicated, starting with port-owned equipment and facilities and evolving to other sources could be advantageous for certain issues. Lower priority issues should be listed in the plan, even if in a general manner, to ensure those issues are tracked for future plan updates and are considered when evaluating programmes and measures related to current efforts. Certain programmes and measures identified to address a priority environmental issue could result in collateral benefits, which are important to consider when evaluating programme options and cost-benefits.

There are several different approaches that can be considered when developing environmental programmes. Several ports have achieved International Organization for Standardization (ISO) 14001 certification for environmental management systems (EMS). The benefits of certification under ISO 14001 are increased assurance of regulatory compliance and a clear process to manage the increasing risk and complexities of environmental management. Although some investment of time and money is needed to develop an environmental management system, there are also potential cost savings. For example, at the Port of Los Angeles (POLA), a hazardous waste reduction programme developed under an EMS programme has increased recycling of latex paint and reduced the cost of handling contaminated bilge water from port owned vessels. This resulted in annual operational savings of over $100,000.

There are ways to ensure that port environmental programmes become embedded in the port management culture and not considered the sole responsibility of environmental staff. Many ports combine their environmental plans or environmental management system with other policies such as green purchasing policies or green building standards into a much larger port-wide sustainability plan. As an example, in 2008 POLA conducted a sustainability assessment that identified 32 specific programmes and policies already in effect at the port. These included:

- Clean air plan
- Water resources action plan
- ISO 14001 certification
- Habitat mitigation policy
- Green building policies
- Climate action plan
- Environmental technology advancement programme

All of the programmes were incorporated into a comprehensive port sustainability plan. This not only established a single reference for all port environmental programmes and policies, but served to clearly illustrate and document POLA's commitment to environmental stewardship on every level. Today it is not uncommon, particularly in ports with a large staff, to find a senior level executive who has the responsibility for sustainability. The higher the responsibility for environmental policy is placed in an organisation, the greater the opportunity for the environmental ethic to be promoted throughout it. Today, senior port officials must be sensitive to, and knowledgeable about, the environmental consequences of their port's operations.

Implementation schedules for various programmes and measures to address environmental issues of concern should be established. Although such schedules may slip, they tend to ensure forward movement. In establishing schedules, it is important to identify those measures that are easy to implement, as this can provide for early successes in plan implementation and can create momentum to carry out the more difficult programmes. Some clear successes early on in the implementation of the plan can often provide a catalyst and generate enthusiasm for the support of future actions and to commit future funding.

Development of metrics to monitor progress of the port's environmental plan is important in evaluating effectiveness, cost benefits and demonstrating improvements to adjacent communities and regulatory agencies. The data used to establish the plan baseline will assist in identifying the appropriate metric to track progress. In some instances, these metrics are based upon calculations such as greenhouse emission reductions. In other cases, the port will need to invest in the periodic collection of monitoring data, such as water quality testing, ambient air quality monitoring and biological surveys. Many ports produce an annual state of the environment report or an annual score card to provide the public with information on how close the port is to achieving its environmental goals.

Available planning tools

Ports and harbours worldwide have implemented various environmental programmes and measures. Furthermore, international ports and harbours have increased coordination and collaboration efforts, resulting in many resources being available to assist in the development of environmental programmes and measures. Some programmes, such as the Environmental Ship Index (ESI) being developed by the

International Association of Ports and Harbours (IAPH), provide for flexible measures that could be used by all ports to promote best practices among port users. A list of a few of the resources and tools available on the web to assist in port environmental plan development includes:

The IAPH website: www.iaphworldports.org provides: a 2011 Survey of Water Quality Issues in ports; how to implement a water quality monitoring programme and other resources.

The World Ports Climate Initiative (WPCI) website: www.wpci.nl was created by IAPH and includes a free air quality and greenhouse gas tool box that provides a menu of emission reduction options that a port could implement. These include onshore power supply, also known as alternative maritime power technology. A carbon foot-printing guide for ports and an associated carbon calculator that can be used by any port is also available.

The European Seaport Association (ESPO) website: www.espo.be provides an environmental code of practice including a handbook of environmental practices and a code of practice on the societal integration of ports. ESPO also manages EcoPorts www.ecoports.com which provides a self-diagnosis method for ports to use in assessing environmental risk and regulatory compliance assisting port in establishing priorities for action.

The American Association of Port Authorities (AAPA) website: www.aapa-ports.org provides a knowledge library under its publication tab that includes several environmental and sustainability studies, reports, papers and resources.

The United States Environmental Protection Agency port compliance tool website: www.portcompliance.org provides an EMS primer for ports, best management practices and green innovations for the port sector, US regulations typical to port facilities, international treaties, and a list of port organisations.

The International Institute for Sustainable Seaports website: http://laurenmoon.com/getf/our-projects-partnerships/the-international-institute-of-sustainable-seaports developed in cooperation with the Global Environmental and Technology Foundation (GETF) and AAPA. The site provides information regarding best practices used at seaports worldwide.

PIANC – The World Association for Waterborne Transport website: www.pianc.org provides high quality technical publications that are available for purchase. Most address dredging and dredge material disposal. But PIANC's Environmental Commission reports cover various port environmental issues. *A Guideline for Sustainable Ports* is currently under development.

The World Organisation of Dredging Associations (WODA) website: www.woda.org is made up of three divisions that cover the globe; abstracts of technical papers, primarily on dredging, are available for free.

Port environmental managers should check these websites frequently or consider membership which can provide more resources and networking opportunities for port environmental managers.

Plan updates

All environmental plans will need periodic review and updating. Changing environmental conditions or new regulations mean that the port's environmental programmes need to adapt to current conditions. As environmental issues and pollution sources are addressed, new issues tend to come to the forefront. The continually changing nature of a port's environmental focus is illustrated by Table 10.1 which shows the top ten environmental issues cited by European sea ports in 1996, 2004, and 2009.

In 1996, water quality and habitat loss were major environmental issues facing the European ports, while air quality was not even listed as one of the top ten priorities. As ports learned to design projects which minimised habitat loss and included habitat restoration elements, the habitat loss issue was overtaken by more pressing issues. Garbage and port waste, noise, and air quality moved up the list. It is likely a future survey will include the production of greenhouse gas emissions as a top ten issue.

Table 10.1 Top 10 Environmental priorities of the European Port Sector

	1996	2004	2009
1	Port development (water)	Garbage and port waste	Noise
2	Water quality	Dredging operations	Air quality
3	Dredging disposal	Dredging disposal	Garbage and port waste
4	Dredging operations	Dust	Dredging operations
5	Dust	Noise	Dredging disposal
6	Port development – land	Air quality	Relationship with local community
7	Contaminated land	Hazardous cargo	Energy consumption
8	Habitat loss or degradation	Bunkering	Dust
9	Traffic volume	Port development – land	Port development – water
10	Industrial effluent	Ship discharges – bilge	Port development – land

(Source: European Sea Ports Organisation (ESPO/ECO) *Ports Review, 2009*)

As measures in a plan are implemented, but additional improvements are identified as still being required, a review of new technologies and other potential sources to control will be required.

Case study

This evolution in environmental issues is further illustrated by the changing nature of the POLA's environmental programmes over the past three decades. Today, those programmes are focused on air pollution and the health risks associated with the emissions of diesel particulate matter (DPM). But in the early 1970s, as industry discharges into ports' waters were largely unregulated, the focus was on water quality. As action was taken and water quality started to improve, the environmental focus changed. In the late 1970s, more cargoes became containerised. This shift necessitated the dredging of larger channels and the creation of land masses for bigger marine terminals.

Environmental concerns shifted to the loss of marine habitats. Then, in the 1980s it became common practice for many ports to develop habitats both inside and outside their port boundaries as mitigation for the impact of port developments. Those efforts continue today but are not considered as remarkable for a port to undertake as they were several decades ago. POLA grew further, and double stacked train operations began to support the expanded container operations. Environmental priorities shifted again, to include rail noise and traffic congestion in the surrounding communities. In the late 1990s, when the State of California declared diesel exhaust to be carcinogenic, the focus shifted to air quality and health risks posed by port operations. This continues to this day.

So while progress is made in addressing specific environmental issues, scientific and health studies continue to identify new contaminates and environmental issues of concern. Therefore, as illustrated in Table 10.1 page 77, attention to priority issues, such as water quality, may decrease in the course of a decade. But with new information it may become a higher priority in a following decade. This demonstrates the potential benefits of port programmes going above and beyond regulatory requirements, as the additional measures or controls can give the port a head start when new contaminates are identified.

Review of environmental plans and policies on a regular basis is important to ensure that actions taken remain pertinent and effective in the ever-changing natural and regulatory environment. Plan updates also provide an opportunity to inform the public on environmental improvements achieved by your port and demonstrate your port's commitment to environmental stewardship and sustainability.

Geraldine Knatz PhD

Executive Director
Port of Los Angeles

In 2006 Geraldine became the first female executive director of the Port of Los Angeles where she oversees the daily operations and internal management of the biggest container port in the USA. The same year, Geraldine was instrumental in the creation and implementation of the San Pedro Bay Ports Clean Air Action Plan which reduced port-related sulphur oxide, diesel particulate matter and nitrogen oxide emission levels by 75%, 69% and 50% respectively between 2005 and 2010. Geraldine has aggressively advanced POLA's 'green growth' agenda, which focuses on clean, sustainable port development, continuous job creation and long-term economic prosperity. Top priorities at the port under her leadership are reducing air emissions, eliminating health risks and expanding capital development programmes to accommodate the port's future growth. Included in *Los Angeles* magazine's Power List of LA influential people, Knatz began a two-year term in May 2011 as the President of the International Association of Ports and Harbors (IAPH), and served as Chair of the American Association of Port Authorities (AAPA) 2008-2009. Geraldine is the recipient of the Blue Frontier Campaign's 2012 Peter Benchley Ocean Award for Excellence in Solutions for her environmental leadership in POLA and in the international greening ports movement.

image: USCG

Chapter 11

The Harbour Master and port safety

By **Alan Coghlan**

Dealing with emergencies is never easy and will cost you sleepless nights. Nevertheless as Harbour Master you will be expected to find a solution to the problems arising from a marine emergency within the port. There is no way of knowing when, where or what may give rise to an emergency. One thing is certain, preparation along the lines discussed in this section will give you, and more importantly, your board, the confidence of knowing you have looked at all eventualities and have an action plan in place to deal with it.

The chapter outlines: tool kit for risk assessment; emergency response equipment; the emergency co-ordination centre; emergency scenarios; port of refuge and the investigation of accidents

Risk assessment tools

The prime function of Harbour Masters is the safety of all marine operations within the jurisdiction of their ports. To achieve a safe port, a Harbour Master must consider what can go wrong and how best to prevent it. This is the underlying principle of risk assessment – a practice that will not only lead to a safer port but may also help to reduce insurance premiums, a commercial benefit to the port company.

There are many proprietary risk assessment tools available on a commercial basis to choose from. It is advisable that the management of the port company agrees to a particular type to use to construct a risk register that may be used to identify all the risks involved in the running of a port. It is also advisable that the tool chosen can be segregated into the functions of the various departments within the port such as corporate, engineering, marine, financial, environment, security and community. Each of the sections should be password protected so that only the managers responsible can have access to their particular areas. The designated Company Risk Officer, which in the case of ports with which I have had experience is normally the Chief Executive, will have access to all sections for the purpose of continuous review and comment.

If your company does not have an official risk register, it is advisable that the marine department conducts its own risk assessment. Of the proprietary risk assessment tools available, some are specifically for the marine aspect of port operations. It is worth noting that a very practical and marine-specific risk assessment tool resulted from the EU MarNis project, completed some years ago. It enables Harbour Masters and pilots to carry out risk assessments based on ship parameters and port parameters. As a stand-alone tool for marine operations within a port it is worthy of consideration.

Fundamental risk assessment

Drilling down into the method and types of risk assessment, it is worth remembering that all of us, whether at sea or in other roles, have always carried out rudimentary risk assessments. How many times in your career have you asked yourself: "If I do this, what is the worst thing that can happen?"

That question is at the very heart of risk assessment. It then must be decided if the expected result of your action is probable or is it more likely that another result will ensue. Having settled on the most likely result you then try to make that result safer to the degree where it is completely safe, or the risk is negligible or at an acceptable level.

All risk assessment tools will be based upon this principle. Multiply the perceived effect or consequence of an event or scenario by the likelihood of that event occurring. The scales used will be numerical and can be as extensive in range as the user may think appropriate. The user will have to decide at what level the result is considered as low as reasonably possible; urgent, requiring immediate action, or moderate requiring a plan to modify the effect. In all systems the goal is to put some mitigating actions that will either reduce the likelihood of, or consequence of an event thereby achieving a safer operation.

Mitigation and planning practices

Risk assessment can be used to plan not only the day-to-day operations of the port, but can be extremely valuable in planning for emergency response and testing the port capability during accidents or disasters. A Harbour Master's concerns extend from collisions to environmental disasters, such as oil or chemical pollution, and loss of life. None of these events are particularly pleasant, as any Harbour Master who has been through them will tell you. If the event is one that is significant enough to reach national or international attention, the person responsible for the day-to-day management of operations and response to the event may well attract blame-orientated attention.

The best insurance against such a reaction is to assess properly the risk of all operations and to put in place reasonable mitigating actions to reduce the risk. If after all that an accident still occurs, you are duty bound to plan for such an event.

Risk assessment tools can be vital in formulating plans suitable for the types of ships calling at your port and to the risks arising from the types of cargoes they carry. Another important factor in determining the eventual type of plan you write is the physical characteristic of the port, including the type of shoreline, tidal regime, flora and fauna, ease of access to the shore and the navigational bottlenecks within your port.

Response equipment considerations

Risk assessment, taking into account the worst credible scenario, will reveal in the risk mitigation phase a list of equipment best suited for response. The assessment will also determine those areas of special conservation or specially protected areas and the measures required to protect those places. It is my opinion that an environmental baseline study of conditions in your port is a very useful exercise. This is particularly so when deciding to what level clean-up or response is required to revert to the baseline conditions that existed prior to an incident.

Having decided, following risk assessment, what response equipment is required, there remains the question of who should purchase and maintain this costly equipment. It will include radios, personal protection equipment, booms, skimmers, recovery craft, response boats, tugs, generators, lights, spray booms, dispersants, cleansing agents, buckets, shovels; the list is almost endless.

In some jurisdictions, where the Harbour Master is an employee of either a local authority, municipality or a state, the responsibility to purchase and maintain the response equipment most likely lies with the employer.

If, on the other hand, a private company employs you, there may be more resistance to outright purchase and maintain such equipment, based on the cost versus the likelihood of its use and cost recovery. In the jurisdiction in which I have been Harbour Master, it was up to each importer, local authority or jetty operator to have a basic level of response capability up to Tier Two depending on the quantity and type of material being imported or exported. This led to a very disjointed approach to provision of response equipment with the inevitable duplication of stocks as each concern merely wished to ensure they had their requirements covered without considering the greater good.

To resolve this in my port, we held a meeting of all the parties involved and suggested that, rather than individual stocks of equipment, we should consolidate all equipment into a central location where stock control, rotation and maintenance could be more economically achieved. All parties readily agreed to this proposal, which in time grew from a mere stock holding system into a full pollution response team with training programmes and stock renewal schedules in place. It was funded by an annual subscription from each of the parties, which proved cheaper to them than individual provision of equipment. As this satisfied all aspects of the legal requirement placed on each operator or stakeholder, the government approved this system. I offer this suggestion based on experience and can vouch for its success.

Initially this system had charitable status, which was tax efficient for each of the contributors, but this soon proved inadequate. In 2001 a vessel capsized during cargo operations with resulting oil pollution to which we responded. Very soon it became evident that we were expending considerable amounts in terms of equipment and personnel with no guarantee of cost recovery. After that lesson the whole system was established as a limited liability company.

Chemical emergencies

Response to an emergency may not, of course, be limited to oil pollution. There are many types of emergency for which you will have to plan. There are emergency concerns around chemicals, both in bulk and in containers. If you are in a port which has a regular trade in chemicals, this will necessitate a carefully planned approach to the transit of ships carrying such goods and where the goods are to be handled within the port estate. Again, I suggest that through careful risk assessment of each of the products, it will become evident who shall respond in the event of an emergency. I say this because in the matter of chemical response, Harbour Masters do not normally have the level of expertise required to control or organise the response. They will be engaged mainly in the control of shipping during such an incident.

Coordinated approach

In dealing with emergencies, a multi-disciplinary approach will be needed to include:

- Fire service
- Ambulance service
- Police
- Port authority, through the Harbour Master

It is vital that the heads of each discipline are situated at the same location during an emergency where full control of events can be achieved through consultation and full sharing of information. It has been my experience that each of those disciplines mentioned may think they are the prime responders and consequently would be unlikely to work at a location other than of their own choosing. That said I still believe that such barriers must be broken down in the best interest of a coordinated approach to controlling and solving the problems presented by the emergency. And these are best agreed to in advance.

An emergency coordination centre will be required to have good communications with the local on-scene controllers. It is not advisable to have personnel from the coordination centre going to the scene in order to establish what is happening before making decisions. The information they require must come to them in a continuous flow so they are fully apprised of dynamic events as they unfold. To ensure this happens each will need to set up their own internal communications systems. These will normally be portable. It is worth recognising that during times of emergency the mobile telephone network will quickly become jammed and is of no value to those responding to the crisis, thereby making discipline specific communication methods vital. A good supply of walkie-talkies with fully charged batteries is worthy of consideration.

There is a question mark over where the emergency coordination centre should be. Taking the obvious view, it should be as close to the emergency as possible. Since the emergency is within the port, the centre should be located within the port. If you are lucky enough to operate a VTS, then I believe the ideal location is in a room in the VTS station. I say this because all the marine information will be available at that location and normally communications can be easily set up at there.

Apart from the requirements of other disciplines you will require charts, meteorological data, tidal data, electronic communications equipment and most important, someone to keep a complete log of events until the emergency is declared over.

Keeping the press informed

Another very important element of emergency control is the use of a dedicated press officer who will deal with all news media enquiries. To do that, the press officer must have access to the emergency control centre. It is advisable that the heads of disciplines agree the information to be given to the press on a regular basis, for example every four hours or so. A proactive approach here is essential. The most important principle in dealing with this subject is giving the press the factual information on a regular basis; otherwise they will print what they believe to be the facts anyway. For more information on this see Chapter 14.

Vital maritime skills

Whether you work for a state, municipality or a private company, the principles will be the same. As Harbour Master you have only one expertise – the safety of ships within the port and all that it entails. You are not an expert in medical triage and evacuation; you are not an expert in firefighting or chemical response. When an emergency arises in a port involving a ship you are a vital cog in the decision-making and control of an emergency: you are part of a team.

Emergency scenarios

When you plan to cope with emergencies it will always pay to consider different scenarios, which will capture the worst things that may happen in a port. This will prompt you to consider how best you can react to the scenario.

A typical group of scenarios may include:

- Collision between two ships resulting in sinking, loss of life and oil pollution
- Fire or explosion on a vessel at anchor or alongside
- Oil pollution following structural failure of ship
- Chemical explosion while discharging a ship
- Release of toxic cloud from a chemical terminal
- Toxic chemical leak from a container on board ship
- Toxic chemical leak from container in stow ashore
- Sinking of a vessel in main channel
- Sinking of a vessel alongside a jetty

- Collision with a jetty
- Ship grounding
- Ships colliding in an anchorage in bad weather
- Leakage from, or damage to, a container holding radioactive material
- Passenger vessel or ferry in collision with another vessel

This list is not exhaustive and will be shaped by the type of port in which you work and the type of trade carried out by the port. As with all things it is far better to be prepared for the worst eventuality and the consideration of scenarios is a very helpful mechanism to concentrate the mind on what could possibly go wrong.

Action plans

The next important step will be to write an action plan for each of the scenarios with the involvement of all the outside response agencies. Their involvement in this process is essential as the input from their perspective will make the plan more practical, efficient and workable. Plans, in my opinion, must not be too prescriptive but must identify those who are responsible for making decisions, where they should be, and in particular what they can make decisions about. There may be legal structures into which you must dovetail a plan; this is more evident in systems that are heavily led by the state or municipality.

There will be obligations on reporting to consider: to government departments such as Coast Guard, national maritime administrations and possibly others. There will be an obligation to have your plans approved by an authority, generally a government. All of this will make it necessary to illustrate that you have considered, together with other response agencies, the possible emergency scenarios that may occur in your port and, more importantly, that you have jointly devised a credible response plan.

Here I would give a warning in relation to plans in general. It is a huge body of work to devise any emergency response plan and the temptation is to think that the job finishes with the plan compilation. There follows a great deal of work in keeping plans up to date in terms of personnel and their contact details, job descriptions and titles. Then you are faced with the need to train in response to any or each of the scenarios in the plan.

Place of refuge

When faced with the decision whether to offer a ship in distress refuge in your port there are a number of crucial pieces of information required. These will apply even if the decision to offer refuge is taken by an authority higher than the port company or the Harbour Master.

Most states in the world have a centrally devised policy. Certainly this is the case for all states in Europe, by EU Directive. The policy has arisen from several incidents around the coast of Europe, where several ports or states have refused entry for fear of pollution. It is now correctly believed that if a ship is brought into a place of refuge where the problem can be contained, even if significant oil pollution ensues, that is preferable and less costly than widespread environmental damage along an extensive part of the coastline from a ship sinking at sea.

Even so you will still need the information to know how best to respond should you be called upon to offer refuge. This requirement will include information on:

- Condition of ship
- Ability to manoeuvre
- Quantity and nature of the cargo if any
- Number and nationality of the crew
- If tug assistance is required
- If anchors are available
- Draught
- Whether there are injured personnel on board
- P & I Club and contact number

That is a basic list of the requirements from a Harbour Masters' perspective and this will allow them to decide how to best deploy their resources to assist with getting the ship into an area best suited to its needs. If the issue is controlled from a national source, they still need to be informed to advise the national controller in the best interest of both the casualty and the port.

Investigations

Following an incident within your port, you may be tasked to conduct an investigation by the board of directors or the Chief Executive. The incident may be a minor issue or an extremely serious one. Nevertheless they all have to be approached with the same respect and undertaken with the same process. Personally I do not believe an investigation should be undertaken to ascertain blame. That may easily become a witch-hunt and the benefits of an investigation are then lost.

The purpose of any investigation must be to:

- Establish the facts surrounding the incident
- Come to a conclusion based on the facts as to how the incident occurred stating the main causal facts
- Make recommendations to improve systems or provide training to prevent a re-occurrence

Always keep an open mind when conducting an investigation, especially when you think the causes are obvious. So never presume, always establish the facts. As part of your investigation you may require written reports from others such as pilots, boatmen, Tug Masters, Shipmasters and staff members. I believe that such reports should be treated as confidential by you as the investigating officer. Such a policy will engender trust and openness amongst those with whom you work and manage. This will make the establishment of the facts less of a trial in the eyes of those directly involved in an incident.

In making recommendations to prevent the same incident from happening again, I strongly suggest you allow input from the persons who will operate similar ships or boats or machinery on a day-to-day basis in the future. Do not exclude those who may have been in charge of an operation during which the incident occurred. This will allow them to demonstrate they have learnt valuable lessons for the future.

If it is the case that an external agency is conducting the investigation in which you are questioned amongst others I can only suggest that you be open, honest and concern yourself with the facts alone. Make no observations nor give opinions, as others will be in charge of that process. If the report makes recommendations about change to either methods or structures, remember you are still the Harbour Master and it will be up to you to establish on behalf of the board whether the recommendations are practicable and whether other suggestions would result in better practice.

Chapter 12

The Harbour Master and incidents

By **Mark Andrews**

Introduction

A Harbour Master's principal role is to try to ensure that all port users are able to go about their business, or leisure, confident that the port environment is being managed with their safety to the fore. But even in the best run ports, whether they are large or small, the Harbour Master can be faced with a crisis.

In such circumstances they will need to be able to respond to the emergency in an appropriate manner. They must swiftly assess what has happened. They need to discover what has unfolded since the incident occurred. They should then respond clearly, decisively and effectively.

Dealing with the media in an emergency is a critical area. Traditionally politicians and the public have been influenced by what the media is reporting. But with the growth of social media, the timescale for ensuring that appropriate messages are communicated has shortened dramatically. Successfully handling such focussed public attention requires an enhanced level of planning and commitment. At times this may detract from the handling of the incident. But trying to ignore the media is not the answer and will nearly always be counter-productive. For more advice on the media, see Chapter 14.

Salvage

Most Harbour Masters will find themselves needing to oversee salvage operations. In the vast majority of cases this will be for minor incidents such as the foundering of a yacht at a mooring or the recovery of cargo or plant that has been lost in the harbour. Such small scale operations are normally competently dealt with by marine contractors that operate within most harbours or can be easily mobilised to a particular harbour.

But Harbour Masters have been faced with major disasters. These could be as severe as the grounding of a large crude carrier and massive pollution of the harbour and adjacent coastline. Such an incident might impact on other countries. The salvage expertise required will almost certainly be beyond local resources and thus require the service of one of the major salvage companies such as those that are members of the International Salvage Union (ISU).

In such situations, the Harbour Master needs to be reassured that the salvor:

- Is competent
- Understands what is required to undertake the salvage
- Has sufficient resources available either on site or deployable within a reasonable timeframe
- Has produced a robust plan

This plan must include such critical points as contingencies, risk assessments and requirements from the port for approval by the Harbour Master.

It should, of course, be borne in mind that for such a major emergency, a Harbour Master is almost certain to be surrounded by, and interface with, a whole range of interested agencies and bodies. Indeed it may also be that even with the Harbour Master's acceptance of any proposal by the salvor, this may in turn need further approval at a higher level such as the UK's SOSREP, or a similar central government authority.

Organisations potentially involved in major casualties include:

- Shipowner
- Salvors
- Emergency services
- SOSREP and salvage advisors
- Local government officials
- National government officials
- Government agencies
- Politicians
- P&I Club
- Underwriters
- Charterers
- Flag State
- Class
- Cargo owner
- Hull and machinery
- ITOPF
- Solicitors, surveyors and investigators for the above
- Legal team and advisors
- Pollution contractors.

Invariably there are significant political and competing pressures from a variety of sources which need to be managed. For example, island communities may be reliant upon lifeline ferry operations. Any casualty or subsequent salvage operation that restricts these has the potential to cause major disruption to that community. Similarly, high value aquaculture businesses may be damaged by even the threat of pollution. Environmental designations such as marine conservation zones (MCZs) also add to the pressures upon the port. In such circumstances, Harbour Masters may consider whether or not they need to obtain independent salvage advice in order to provide a peer review of the salvor's plan. But salvage is a specialist business and independent advice could of course lead to conflicting opinion on the best course of action.

Port of refuge

Vessels of every size and shape use the sea for a variety of reasons and may find themselves in a distressed state; perhaps from a shift of cargo or water ingress. In such circumstances vessels seek out a port of refuge. In reality this can be any place that provides safety for the particular vessel. A safe haven will provide an area where the reason for the distress may be addressed and allow the voyage to be resumed. Most Harbour Masters find themselves being approached to accept such a vessel. The main impact upon emergency planning is that such a request could come from a passing vessel which would not ordinarily trade to the port. Clearly this brings about an added complication. For example, for a pure tanker port, it may struggle to handle a large container ship or a car carrier.

Indeed there may be a temptation, as evidenced through a number of high profile incidents such as the *Castor* and *Erika*, to refuse entry to the port to vessels in distress on the basis that the ports have a duty to protect their harbours. While this may be an easy option, it may or may not be the best one for the vessel in distress, its crew and the environment.

However, other factors can sometimes influence the decision. For example, in the UK under the Water Resources Act 1991, it is a strict liability offence to pollute water courses, including harbour areas. If a Harbour Master allows a vessel in distress into the port and that vessel has a subsequent pollution, then both the Harbour Master and the port authority are automatically guilty of an offence unless:

- It involved the safety of life
- Pollution was minimised
- The UK Environment Agency was notified of the pollution

This seems straightforward. But if the crew could have been evacuated by helicopter or lifeboat prior to entry then relying on safety of life is not an acceptable defence. In the UK, the maximum penalty is an unlimited fine and/or up to two years in prison.

Responding to an emergency

In deciding how to respond to any emergency, the size and complexity of the port plays a significant part. A large port will probably have a VTS centre operating on a 24/7 basis. It will have the skills and expertise to be able to undertake appropriate assessment of emergencies and will activate the port's emergency plans. In a small port there may be no VTS and a notification will need to be forwarded to the Harbour Master via an emergency notification system. For example, for a small municipal port, through the local authority emergency call response system.

Response

Emergencies frequently involve a considerable number of agencies and organisations that need to cooperate and provide support to each other. Ideally each nation should have some form of generic national framework for managing emergency responses. This is applicable, irrespective of the nature, scale or cause of a particular event. Using the UK as an example, a three-tiered system is used within which individual agencies or organisations can develop their own response and recovery plans. Management effort is undertaken at one or more of the following levels:

Bronze – operational level

This level is at the coalface of the incident. Personnel first on scene will assess the immediate steps necessary dependent upon the nature and scale of the incident. Those in charge will concentrate on specific tasks within their own areas of responsibility. For example, a pilot may be reporting back to the VTS on the current status aboard the vessel. The port officer, responding to the scene, may establish an exclusion zone around the area. Separately, a fire and rescue service commander may begin deployment of assets. Agencies retain control of their own response resources and personnel, but must cooperate to ensure a coherent and integrated effort. In many instances these arrangements will be adequate enough to deal with most emergencies.

Silver – tactical level

The purpose of the silver level is to ensure that actions taken at the bronze level are coordinated, coherent and integrated to achieve maximum effectiveness and efficiency. It is usually comprised of the most senior personnel for each agency committed to the area of operations; silver assumes the tactical command of the situation and, in particular, will:

- Determine resource allocation priorities
- Plan and co-ordinate how and when tasks will be undertaken
- Obtain additional resources, if required
- Assess significant risks and use these to inform tasking of bronze commanders
- Ensure health and safety of public and personnel

Gold – strategic level

Where an event or situation has very substantial resource implications or is tasking for an extended duration, it may be necessary to implement multi-agency management at the gold level.

This is particularly necessary if there are long-term implications for the environment, local communities and the economy. Gold assumes responsibility for the multi-agency management of the emergency. It will decide the policy and strategic framework within which silver will work. Specific duties are:

- Determine, promulgate and review both a clear strategic aim and objectives
- Establish a policy framework for the event
- Prioritise the demands of silver and allocation of resources to meet them
- Formulate and implement media handling and public communication plans
- Direct planning and operations beyond response to recovery operations

Record keeping

It is vital that appropriate records are kept from the initial event, how it developed and how and why responses were adopted or modified over the duration of the emergency. Such records are essential, both to justify internally or to be able to claim against insurers or a claim fund.

Indeed, at the height of any incident the restraint on spending may appear to be absent. But unless the justification is robust, there will be significant arguments about whether or not such expenditure was absolutely necessary.

Records are also essential to assist in the post-incident recovery phase. They will primarily teach lessons in how to reduce the likelihood of the event happening again and also to check the veracity of the emergency plan itself and modify it where necessary.

Withdrawal strategy

In most instances an emergency will have an obvious conclusion and in such circumstances operations will logically cease. But in other incidents, particularly those involving prolonged pollution, the withdrawal strategy will be more complicated. But it is important that continued communication and agreement with other interested agencies need to be reached.

Investigations and claims

In major events, a number of significant investigations into the cause will take place. The purpose is to establish a clear set of facts as to what happened and why. They will enable lessons to be learnt and identify if any further recourse is necessary. Legal outcomes of criminal acts such as oil pollution or breaches of port regulations and also civil claims take a long time to materialise. They take longer still to come to a resolution, either through an out-of-court settlement or court ruling.

Information gathering

When a salvor arrives on scene it is more than likely that the port's emergency response has been activated. It will be undertaking a holding operation while the specialist knowledge and expertise of the appointed salvors is deployed. Naturally the salvors will need to be briefed on how the incident unfolded, the current situation and resources both deployed and available. But the port must also obtain information to enable it to understand what plans have been activated, their hierarchy and most importantly who is in charge.

12.1 Hierarchy of responsibility	
Responsibility	
Whose plan is it?	**Specific:** Small port and harbour Terminal Refinery Offshore platform **General:** Ports and harbour with many operators North Sea National plan eg UK Contingency Plan Regional agreement eg Humber estuary plan International agreement eg Bonn Agreement (North Sea States)
Who has responsibility?	Federal command State control Facility Manager Harbour Master Other or combination
Scope	What area does the plan cover? What is its geographical boundary? What has to be protected? How does the plan link in with other plans and agreements? What resources are available?

Who is ultimately responsible depends very much on the country in which either the incident has occurred or to which the casualty has been taken. But a limited survey conducted through the International Harbour Masters Association reveals that generally speaking, port assets are controlled by a port official, normally the Harbour Master or port manager. The overall responsibility lies with government either through a civil servant or a politician. Some examples below:

12.2 Overall responsibility

Country	Port Official	Ultimately responsible
UK	Harbour Master	Secretary of State's Representative (SOSREP)
Germany	Harbour Master	Havariekommando (equivalent to SOSREP)
Belgium	Port Commander	Governor
Israel	Port Manager	Ministry of Environment
Gibraltar	Harbour Master	Harbour Master (has SOSREP powers)
Australia	Harbour Master	Maritime Emergency Response Commander (MERCOM)
New Zealand	Harbour Master	Chief Executive, Maritime New Zealand

Media/public relations

By definition, a full scale incident will happen suddenly and develop at breakneck speed. Ports need to be able to oversee the emergency response, and handle the media as well. This has been touched upon in the introduction, but it is a vital topic.

There will invariably be a structure in place where a senior manager has responsibility for following the response that others are making to an emergency. They will dedicate themselves to putting in place the key communications network. They will be an integral part of regular emergency planning meetings during an incident, as they will need to have access to information first hand to turn into statements and updates.

The key message to be contained within these statements should be that the port is working with the wider response group to contain the situation. It is in control of what's happening and is anticipating and preparing for likely developments.

Public health and safety information will also be a prominent feature of the statements.

The impact of social media has meant that the timescale to respond is now much less than it was and there is huge pressure for continually providing appropriate information. This requires constant feedback from the incident site. Waiting an hour for the next briefing is no longer an option as video from mobile phones is transmitted around the world in seconds. A salvage company representative needs to be permanently located within the port command team in constant contact with a salvage Master at the casualty. This is often a salvage manager. Given the 24/7 nature of major disasters, this requires considerable resources up-front which may be scaled back if and when the situation settles down. But even then, events such as weather or further damage can resurrect and heighten an emergency.

Death or serious injury

Where an emergency has led to the death or serious injury of employees, details of such incidents will be released only by the police. They will only release personal details after next of kin have been informed and any media enquiries relating to such matters must, at all times, be referred to them.

Conclusion

The essence of successfully managing an emergency lies in planning, training, exercising and reviewing the relevant emergency plan. Given the circumstances of major incidents, the intensity of public interest, political scrutiny and the need to maintain customer confidence, the reality is that patience is short and any other agencies working with the Harbour Master, such as salvage companies, must be able to provide timely information. A joint approach to those ultimately in authority is more likely to be approved. For this to work considerable mutual trust is required; not easy when dealing with strangers. Finally, the media aspect requires sensitive management but, from a port perspective, the message will be: "we are in control of the situation and are responding appropriately".

This Chapter appears in similar form in The Nautical Institute's book, *Casualty Management Guidelines.*

Captain Mark Andrews MNI
Harbour Master
Milford Haven

ABOUT THE AUTHOR

Mark Andrews served at sea in the UK merchant navy for 13 years on a variety of vessel types. He took a second career ashore, firstly as a VTS Officer, then as a pilot before returning to port management ultimately becoming Milford Haven Harbour Master in 1995.

He has experienced a number of incidents throughout his career beginning with a stove-in hatch during a storm on his first trip to sea. Others included fires, groundings, collisions, foundering, berthing damage, cargo losses and oil pollution. Most were dealt with without the need for external assistance and where help was required, for example to recover a barge foundered on moorings, the services of a local contractor were adequate for the task.

He experienced the 1995 grounding of the double hull tanker *Borga* and in 1996, the single hull tanker *Sea Empress*, as Harbour Master. These were of an altogether different scale and required an international multi-agency response.

He continues in his role as Harbour Master and is a past president of the UK Harbour Masters' Association.

Chapter 13

The Harbour Master and the local community

By **Captain Sean Bolt** BA M.Prof Stud. FCILT

Welcome to your new role as Harbour Master. You will have been employed for the qualifications you hold, combined with your nautical knowledge and seagoing experience. However, the corporate environment you find yourself in, and especially some of the requirements that will be placed upon you to interact with the community, may well be an entirely new prospect for you. It will be an experience for which you will have received little advice or no training. I hope the following information may be of some assistance in identifying with whom you will need to engage and why.

The Harbour Master's role will vary according to local custom and the regulatory framework. It will primarily exist for, and generally cover, the safety of the port environment as well as the safety of commercial shipping that uses the port. It may extend, depending on legislation, to cover all recreational water activity, not only in the port, but over a wide geographical area or even region.

The traditional role of the Harbour Master is changing. It now encompasses a number of roles beyond that of controlling the safety of commercial shipping, the regulation of port activities and overall responsibility for pilotage standards and examination.

Ports, along with most large businesses, are expected to engage with stakeholders to varying degrees, in an open and honest manner. We should examine those stakeholder groups, presented in no particular order or level of importance.

Stakeholder groups include:

- Shareholders
- Customers
- Ships and their crews
- Employees
- Management
- Directors
- Service providers
- Labour unions
- Central government such as ministries of transport, planning and/or marine departments
- National maritime safety organisations

- National oil pollution agencies
- National port security agencies
- Quarantine protection agencies
- Customs and border control agencies
- Immigration agencies
- Accident investigation agencies
- Market regulators, such as anti-monopoly and anti-corruption agencies
- Stock exchanges (for listed ports)
- Regional, district and local councils
- Naval establishments
- Shipping agents
- And finally, the community

Much can be written about the importance of each of the stakeholder groups and their roles and responsibilities and how they interact with a port. I will concentrate in this chapter on the Harbour Master's role in engaging with the diverse interest groups that make up the 'local community'.

I use the word engaging specifically. In a modern world it is not the role of the Harbour Master to dictate to members of the community what they can and can't do on the water and what restrictions the port may or may not impose. The expectation from these groups is that there will be a consultation process where their desires and concerns are listened to, and if possible, accommodated. This does not mean that as Harbour Master you don't have the final say – that may be determined by statute or regulation. But where appropriate or practicable, their requirements or concerns should be considered. The Harbour Master must ensure an open communication process with the other senior employees of the port and establish where and to whom the responsibility for engaging with each stakeholder group will lie.

The diverse interest groups that the label 'community' covers are listed below. The list may not be exhaustive, but covers some of the groups to whom the author has had exposure.

The community generally may include a number of different parties, and can be broken down into a number of sub-groups.

Port and harbour users

These will be groups that use the port and harbour environment, whose activities are affected by the ports operational constraints and to a degree may impact on the safety of port operations – especially the safe movement of vessels. The list covers both commercial and recreational activities and includes:

- Fisherman, both commercial and recreational
- Yacht and power boat clubs
- Diving clubs
- Sea scouts

- Naval cadets
- Kayakers and canoeists
- Kite surfers
- Wind surfers
- Surfers
- Rowing clubs
- Tourist operators
- Ferry operators
- Sea plane operators
- Water ski clubs
- Jet ski operators
- Marina operators
- The public

Without going through each group and attempting to describe their individual requirements, suffice it to say that each of these groups will have specific needs and desires. They are either interested in different parts of the harbour or activities that are undertaken at certain times of the year. For example, international yacht regattas on a specific date may impose on commercial shipping activities.

As Harbour Master you should consider those requirements and if possible, and where appropriate, make arrangements that allow for those activities. The activities may be constrained geographically, or to certain times of the day, or days of the week. They may take place at certain times of the year, or be constrained by other operational requirements which can be set in consultation with affected parties. The key is to have an open mind, as each of these activities will be very important to those that follow them. Likewise, the disruption and or safety issues that arise from those activities will need to be diplomatically conveyed to each of those affected groups. If necessary, and as a last resort, specific legislation such as health and safety, port security, harbours Acts, pilotage Acts, marine pollution etc can be quoted to defend a non negotiable position adopted by the Harbour Master. But when quoting legislation, ensure you understand it and that it is appropriate to the circumstances.

The degree to which each party can affect the activities of other parties or commercial port operations will need careful thought and discussion with the port management. Any final decision will need to be conveyed to the interest group and communicated to other affected parties.

Special interest groups

These are groups that have an active interest in the operations of the port. These are mainly landside and their interests lie in its impact on the environment and the immediate residents, who may play an active and sometimes vocal role in monitoring that the port complies with regulatory and statutory responsibilities. These include:

- Quality of air
- Quality of water
- Quality of lifestyle
- Noise pollution
- Visual pollution
- Traffic impact of road and rail

Groups with an active interest in port operations include:

- Residents and ratepayers
- Noise control groups
- Environmental protection groups
- Business associations
- Dredging monitoring groups

Powers of enforcement of ports' obligations will come from regulations set by regional councils or by state governments. It is imperative that the port engages with these groups. It should explain any major changes to operations or major infrastructure developments and how the port intends to meet its regulatory obligations. For the Harbour Master, this may include how access to the port is controlled, the regulation of noise from stevedoring operations and ships generators and both air and visual pollution from poorly maintained ships' main engines.

Welfare agencies

These are very important groups and must be afforded maximum possible access to visiting ships. Please remember that in many ports, visiting ships crews have a legislative right to go ashore to access labour organisations, fresh food, medical advice, recreation and spiritual guidance.

These include:

- Stella Maris
- Mission to Seafarers
- Mariner's Welfare Societies
- Other entities assisting foreign seafarers while in port

Emergency services

These are local groups that will play a key role in the event of an emergency in the port and include:

- Police
- Firefighting personnel
- Ambulance crews
- Hospital staff

- Coast Guard personnel
- Sea rescue or lifeboat personnel
- Civil defence personnel, in the event of earthquake, flooding, tsunami, or bush fires
- Health and safety inspectors
- Oil pollution operators

The Harbour Master will be required to liaise with these organisations and the port may have standard operating procedures in the event of an identified emergency. This will include contact details for key personnel in each of the organisations along with a description of each person's role and level of responsibility.

Other important stakeholders

While not directly part of the community, although they may be, other groups the Harbour Master will have close association with are state and federal agencies.

These include:

- Maritime safety
- Customs
- Quarantine
- Maritime accident investigation agencies
- Port security agencies

It is important that the Harbour Master has a working relationship with a contact person from each of these agencies to seek guidance from and exchange information.

Mediums to exchange information

There are a number of different mediums by which information can be disseminated and important issues raised and discussed.

These include:

- Open public meetings
- Private meetings
- Group e-mail
- Private e-mail
- Formal letters
- Newsletters
- Advertising by print, radio or television
- Websites
- Newspaper articles
- Magazine articles
- Notices to mariners (temporary and permanent)
- Links to social media such as Facebook and Twitter

What is important is that any issue is clearly defined, the potential problems that arise are listed and how and what the port intends to do to remove, reduce or mitigate any detrimental issues. Any provided information and or data must be factual.

Any public statements will normally have to comply with the port's policy on who is responsible and allowed to make public comment. In some companies this is restricted to the Chairman or the CEO only. A word of warning must be sounded here. Going on television requires training to obtain the best affect. For public interviews for radio, press or television, it is wise to ask for and receive a list of the questions that will be asked and to stick to a script. Some journalist will allow you to view an article before it is published. It is important to ask for this. If the issue is contentious, it is relatively easy for a journalist to interpret what you say in a negative way. For more discussion of media issues please see Chapter 14.

Captain Sean Bolt BA M.Prof Stud. FCILT

Harbour Master
Albany Australia

ABOUT THE AUTHOR

Sean went to sea in 1976 as a cadet with the Union Steam Ship Company of New Zealand obtaining a Second Mate's Foreign Going Certificate in 1979. His seagoing experience included general cargo ships, tankers, bulkers and ro-ro vessels in the Australasian and Pacific Islands area. He obtained his Foreign Going Master's Certificate in 1990.

In addition he holds a Bachelor of Arts from Auckland University and a Masters of Professional Studies (endorsed Transport) from Lincoln University. He has held a variety of senior maritime positions including CEO of a port authority, CEO of a shipping company and CEO of a stevedoring and marshalling company.

He has been a licensed pilot at the New Zealand ports of Tauranga and Westport where he was also the Harbour Master. Currently he is the Harbour Master, and an approved unrestricted pilot, at the port of Albany in Western Australia.

Chapter 14

The Harbour Master and the media

By **James Herbert**

Aided by spiders' webs of modern communication networks, the media is an ever present force. But, with the right approach, its power can be influenced, redirected and used to our advantage. Added to this is the viral influence of the digital age – everyone, it seems, has a camera on their mobile phone and is not afraid to use it. The world is truly a public place; no-one can escape scrutiny, however remote the incident.

Reputation management

Major incidents in all spheres of business have the capacity to destroy in hours the reputation that a port has taken perhaps decades to build. The maritime industry is one that is particularly exposed to reputational threats. There are inherent risks in the operation of vessels and the impact of a shipping incident can be far-reaching with real human, environmental and financial consequences far beyond the impact on those directly connected with the vessel involved in the incident. Furthermore, shipping disasters are often highly visual and images associated with casualties carry a power beyond words.

In most parts of the world the public lacks confidence in the conduct of those in the corporate sector or public authorities. Numerous past scandals and examples of poor behaviour or poor practice mean that responders must work hard to be believed and for their messages to be accepted by the public. All those involved will be subjected to intense scrutiny.

Despite the obvious potential threat to reputation, many fail to prepare properly for the possibility of major public interest in an incident. The result of such failure is loss of control of the public dimension to the incident, which can rapidly turn a major incident into a crisis. The worst outcome could even be the withdrawal of an entity's 'licence to operate', whether through formal action by the authorities, or by the informal withdrawal of support and business by customers and other stakeholders.

From the outset of any major incident, therefore, effective management of communication with stakeholders must be at the heart of the response effort. That communication will only be effective if the management and response systems have been well-planned and practised and include robust media and stakeholder engagement.

There are several strands to the response effort which must work harmoniously together in their response to media and public interest. The on-site team, which may include the Harbour Master, other port and maritime administration officials, representatives of shipping companies, Shipmasters and crews of any vessel involved, local agents and outside agencies such as salvors. Views from other, senior management from port or terminal head offices, government officials or shipping companies plus representatives involved in the response to medical or pollution incidents may also have to be considered. As the incident unfolds it may be appropriate for senior managers from these organisations to move to the port to take charge of the response effort and to be available for engagement with media and other stakeholders.

Rapid escalation

A major incident can become a major public issue extremely rapidly. Depending on the circumstances it may be some time before the incident begins to generate public and media interest but once that happens the level of pressure on media responders can increase from zero to the extreme in a matter of minutes when the story 'breaks'. There will not be time to start developing plans and response systems and if the team is not prepared and drilled it will quickly lose control and be prey to negativity. During a major incident that has attracted international interest it is possible that the response team may be fielding many hundreds of press enquiries each day.

The internet, social media and the citizen journalist

Anyone with a modern mobile phone can take pictures and video footage and post it rapidly on the internet. It means that even in remote parts of the world there is a strong likelihood that images of the incident will be available long before the traditional media deploys its news-gathering resources.

The cruiseship *Costa Concordia*, which hit rocks off the Italian coast in January 2012, is a prime example. The incident occurred in the evening and by daybreak the world's screens were filled with footage of the incident, much of it taken by passengers. It was accompanied by damaging commentary informed by speculation. Bloggers and users of social media will circulate opinion and information about an incident rapidly and informally but with potentially great impact. Social media can also be a source of news 'leads' based on revealing content; for example, from family members of those involved in the incident.

The blame culture seeks instant evidence, there is trial by media, and conclusions are drawn within hours of the incident.

Increased competition between media outlets drives an increasing demand for news. It also increases the demands on responders as the hunger for information and interviewees will be very great. But that provides an opportunity as well.

The 'information vacuum' is there to be filled. It can be filled with rumour, speculation, the voices of critics or it can be filled with messages and material chosen and provided by the port and its responders. And increasing demand for information means that the media will be receptive to what responders have to say.

The media

News media continue to evolve rapidly. The late 20th century and early 21st century witnessed an explosion in the number of media outlets in line with the expansion of the internet. It has had a profound effect on the communications element of managing an incident.

Scrutiny is continuous and more intense; there is more coverage of the incident; national borders (as well as cultural borders) are broken down and the time of day is irrelevant. It is always 'prime time' somewhere. The appetite for rolling 24-hour news is insatiable and the incident will, in many cases, be played out in real-time. Small details and events will be analysed and have the potential to take the incident in different directions. Newswires operate in real time and are in many ways the most important media, given that the stories which they file will be the chief source of news for other media. Newswires also have a reputation for accurate and fair reporting.

Television

While there is a distinction between general news, rolling news, documentary teams, regional TV and national and international operators they all share one thing. They need pictures. The more dramatic the pictures the more prominence the story might be given. They also need interviewees and will seek out anyone with authority to comment and through 'vox pops', anyone at all who has a view on the issue.

Radio

This is fast and responsive with limited technical back-up required to file complex stories.

Traditional print

Newspapers and magazines; the growth of electronic news media has weakened the importance of the 'news' element of traditional print media. By the time consumers read the print media they are probably well aware of the incident from other sources. But the print media has a much greater capacity for news analysis, features and editorial comment making them extremely potent as opinion leaders for both the public and for officials. They also have mass circulation which of itself generates political pressure – particularly if a paper launches a 'campaign'. Most operate an internet news service, however, usually using a mix of their own resources and newswires.

Media handling principles

It is essential right from the start that information provided by Harbour Masters or their media teams is accurate and is based on known facts. This is particularly important if there are injuries or fatalities. Speculation must be avoided. Nothing must be issued publicly unless it is true. It can mean that there is not much to say in the early stages and so there is a need for generic information at this stage. The key is to establish the port as the authoritative source of information about the incident and maintain that credibility through a regular flow of meaningful information. Nothing substantive should be hidden, even if it is damaging. It will eventually be found out and the consequences will be worse. In short, the public accepts that accidents happen. It does not accept that it should be misled. Timing the release of damaging material is important, and should be accompanied by suitable preparation to deal with the additional interest it will create.

For all the changes in the media, the fundamentals of journalism have not altered and the principles of successful and safe engagement with the media during a major incident remain the same.

The objective of good media handling is simple: To find the right balance between cooperating with and understanding the demands of the media and protecting the interests of the port. The right balance and good relationships will lead to fairer coverage of the incident.

In striking the right balance, responders should recognise that journalism is, in most cases, a commercial enterprise with a product to sell and that 'good news' is not necessarily attractive. The media will almost always be intrusive and too aggressive for the port's taste; it is unrealistic to expect glowing coverage even if the incident is being well handled. And business leaders can be the architects of their own downfall by being defensive, unprepared and poor communicators.

The media typically want news:

- A strong story
- Conflict
- Emotion
- The big and powerful wrong or at fault
- A cause

Regardless of the nature of the incident, reporters will always want to know specifics of the incident:

- What happened?
- Why, where, when?
- Are there injuries or fatalities?
- Who is to blame?
- What is the port doing about it and when?
- What are the costs?

At the same time there will be generic questions about the industry; two examples might be safety standards and records, and a lack of concern for the environment.

Planning and preparation

Any organisation engaged in activities that carry some risk to life, the environment, property or its own business should have in place an up-to-date major incident management plan. The plan must be well-understood and available to all those who might need it and it must be rehearsed or drilled regularly. It must contain direction on how to handle the media in an incident.

The features of such a plan are:

- Short and simple
- Readily useable format
- Available to all who need to use it
- Regularly updated
- Incorporate lessons learned from incidents in the maritime and other industries

Typically it will include:

- An introduction outlining the scope of the plan in the context of the business
- An explanation of the escalation process by which those in the chain of command are informed of the incident and the decision-making process to determine the required response
- An explanation or schematic of the organisation of the incident response team
- Checklists of immediate actions for the various roles in the team
- Guidelines on media handling, which should include the method by which potentially high volumes of media enquires will be safely handled
- Guidelines on communicating with relatives of those involved which must cover the possibility of serious injuries and fatalities. This should be kept separate from the media response effort
- The process for managing the flow of information, gaining approval and disseminating public information
- An explanation of what locations and resources will be used to manage the crisis
- An up-to-date and accessible contact list for all key players and their alternates

In addition to the response plan there should be readily available key information about the port, its trade, its staff, its safety record and so on. Suitable pictures in high resolution should be available to be issued to the media as appropriate.

Training

The major incident management plan will be useless if left on the shelf. Staff should be trained to understand the plan and their part in it. it should be stress-tested and practised using realistic scenarios. Such training must have the commitment of all key individuals and senior management. The frequency of training is clearly a matter for the port to decide but it is considered that anything less than an annual drill will be inadequate. Training and practise in media handling is essential.

Media handling in a crisis – the key points

Understand the principles of producing an effective media statement

Issue statements as soon as possible and add to them as more information becomes available. Ensure statements only contain known facts. Statements should deal with human consequences first; details such as injuries or fatalities, then the environment and what is being done to manage the incident. Demonstrate your concern. Property and financial consequences are not a priority. Use background information and positive generic messages to fill the information vacuum. Do not speculate and do not apportion blame.

A standard statement may include:

- Statement number and time and date
- What has happened
- Where
- Deaths and injuries
- Actions being taken
- The weather or other environmental matters of note
- A quote from a senior manager, if available and appropriate
- Pre-prepared, relevant background information
- Contact details

Do not:

- Name human casualties unless cleared to do so – especially if deaths are involved as the police may release names in that case
- Refer to causes or apportion blame
- Estimate costs or compensation issues
- Release any information which has not been approved according to the process set out in the plan

Do:

- Be responsive to the media; return calls and be sure to have enough trained staff, or an outsourced team, to handle high volumes of media interest in the incident
- Correct inaccurate reporting, but do not be evasive, defensive or aggressive with media. Bad news will find its way out, so issue it on your terms
- Ensure that spokespeople are identified and have been trained to handle media interviews and press conferences
- Know where you would hold a press conference and how to stage one
- Update the port website quickly and out of normal office hours

Channels of communication:

- Media statement (as explained before and regularly updated)
- Website updates
- The press conference
- The broadcast interview

If the location of the incident is accessible and its duration is protracted, the centre of gravity of the port response will shift to the site of the incident. In these circumstances senior management from the port are likely to have deployed to the location.

The decision to hold a press conference will depend to a large extent on the numbers of media present at the location, the availability of senior staff to lead the conference and the quality and quantity of information available. The conference will usually be chaired by a professional media advisor who will introduce the participants. These should be relevant senior figures from the port. The most senior figure will give a brief statement and will then take questions from the floor moderated by the chair. Likely questions should have been anticipated, answers prepared and practised. An effective strategy for closing the session in a dignified way without a scrum developing must be planned and executed.

Broadcast media interviews

Choice of interviewee is a key element and nobody should conduct a broadcast interview without prior training. Messages and answers should be kept simple and any tendency to be angry or argumentative must be suppressed. The interviewee must be fully briefed and knowledgeable about the incident. in a protracted incident the demands of regular broadcast interviews will be great and can come to dominate the spokesman. Recognise the difference between a live and a pre-recorded interview. In many cases a live interview will offer the better opportunity to put across positive messages. Pre-recorded interviews will be edited and converted into programming later so be careful about comments taken 'out of context'.

Consistency of message and messaging

Throughout all communications, consistency of message is essential. The information and statements given to different sets of stakeholders may be packaged differently but the content must be the same. it is also essential that there is coordination between all the different organisations party to the incident and that there is agreement on the content of communications.

In practice, gaining such agreement may be difficult as there will be tension and different requirements. Managing relationships with others in the wider response effort is crucial in ensuring a good outcome.

The incident response model adopted in the USA reinforces this consistency by establishing a Joint information Centre made up of all relevant parties under the direction of the incident commander and through which all public communication is channelled.

Behaviour and gaffes

It is vital that all those connected with the response recognise that for the duration of the incident they are in the spotlight and never off duty. No one should engage with media without authorisation and those authorised should not make any unprepared or 'off the cuff' statements. Jokes and seemingly light-hearted banter can be devastating.

There are numerous examples of casual comment causing offence and damaging the reputation of the individual and the port. One is never off-duty and caution should be exercised in all conversations. Nothing is properly 'off the record'. Ever.

Conclusion

It is entirely possible to engage safely and effectively with the media and in so doing, provide a necessary service to the public. The public has a right to know what has happened and what is being done about it. But such engagement is only likely to be successful if it has been thought through in advance; plans have been created and staff have been trained and tested in realistic drills. The level of pressure will escalate rapidly.

This has to be experienced to be understood. early release of accurate information; early 'fronting up' by senior staff; working with media rather than against them; keeping up a flow of information and being responsive will help protect your hard-won reputation.

This Chapter appears in similar form in The Nautical Institute's book, *Casualty Management Guidelines*.

James Herbert
Managing Director Gem Communications Limited

ABOUT THE AUTHOR

James is a former British army officer who became a newspaper and broadcast journalist. He was an award winning producer of current affairs programmes for the BBC before joining energy giant Shell where he became global head of media relations. There he gained much experience with the handling of communications for major incidents and shipping casualties.

James joined the UK's Department of Health as director of communications for one of its major divisions and now runs a corporate communications consultancy providing advice and services to a number of significant clients.

Chapter 15

The Harbour Master and rules and regulations

Case study: border control and the illegal trafficking of migrants in the Mediterranean region

By **Captain Rueben Lanfranco**
BA (Crim) M Jur (Int Law) LL M (IMLI) Dip Mar Sur AMRINA MIFireE MCILT AFRIN FNI FIIMS MIM

The subject of border control encompasses virtually every known aspect of security and safety-related issues connected with a State's shoreline and the adjoining sea. Thus it may directly involve a Harbour Master's area of jurisdiction. Border control may involve both military and civil policing operations and is aimed primarily at preventing illicit activity, which may affect the security and safety of a State. In most cases, border control is primarily associated with curtailing the illicit trafficking of people, which causes a direct violation of the State's immigration laws. Ports are vulnerable areas, as most illegal migrants discovered and recovered at sea will invariably be disembarked at a port, thus adding to the responsibilities of the Harbour Master.

A common incident, especially in Mediterranean ports, might involve Harbour Masters being informed that a vessel is heading for port with as many as 250 illegal migrants who have been picked up from a sinking boat. This is where things might start getting complicated.

First it is imperative that the Harbour Master should have a very good working relationship with other organisations and entities that might be expected to be involved in such cases. These could include those working in the port or harbour area, such as port security personnel, pilots and mooring personnel or tug operators who may assist the safe mooring of the vessel. It also might include other authorities such as the police, medical staff, immigration authorities, Coast Guard, diplomatic or consular representatives and the media.

A secure place in the port or harbour must be identified for the safe disembarkation of the illegal migrants which will allow for a triage area to be set up to screen the migrants. They will need to be checked out medically and provided with adequate food and drink before further action is taken.

The location should be secured so no unauthorised people gain admittance to the area and there should be suitable controls for the access and egress of both people and vehicles. Vehicular access should to allow for a two-way flow of traffic to the triage area and adequate space for a vehicle mustering or a parking area, especially for ambulances and other authorised vehicles.

Such a setup should not affect the operation of other vessels in port but should be designed to function independently of all other operations taking place at the time, whether by day or night. The Harbour Master may have in place contingency plans for such an eventuality but it is imperative that there are regular exercises, at least once or twice a year, by all parties concerned. It may also be beneficial to ensure that a common incident management and command structure is in place and that a room or designated area close to the area of operations is reserved to be used as an incident command post (ICP).

Harbour Masters should also ensure that they have, where possible, other people available who are adequately trained to liaise with other organisations and coordinate the disembarkation of the migrants.

Key points:

This operation will take many hours, adding to the fatigue of Harbour Masters should they be managing this on their own

Harbour Masters should preferably be situated in a central ICP from where they may control and manage the operation. If the ICP is not directly in the area of operations, some form of video link system could be installed in the port or harbour to assist the incident team. It needs to know what is actually taking place in the area close to the vessel disembarking the migrants via the video link.

Harbour Masters should not make the mistake of going on board the vessel and remaining there while migrants disembark. This could mean that they are not in control of what is happening elsewhere in the port or harbour.

Communications are of the utmost importance so have available a quantity of fully-charged handheld radios with a common frequency. These should be distributed to the heads of the various organisations involved in the operation such as the police, health and immigration officials. This will facilitate communications and save having to go through a complicated system to contact individuals to coordinate operations. Mobile phones are useful, but sometimes their use during such operations is not that effective and reception may be limited inside the hull of a vessel or close to large port structures.

Incident management should be well established and frequently exercised to ensure that it actually works. Harbour Masters need to work to the requirements of the ISPS Code and any other domestic legislation which may be in force in their jurisdiction.

Safety should be of prime concern as most people involved with the processing of migrants may not be familiar with potential dangers in the port or harbour area. They will need a safety briefing prior to arriving on site. This should be possible because in most cases any vessel picking up migrants from the sea will give advance notification of her intention to enter port to disembark them. This should provide ample time for responding organisations to arrive on site in the designated disembarkation area and set up the required reception facilities in advance.

Adequate arrangements should be in place to avoid the possibility of migrants jumping ship whilst the vessel is still underway inside the port or harbour. A Coast Guard or police vessel closely escorting the ship carrying the migrants would, in most cases, act as a deterrent for migrants planning such action.

Only allow the vessel into port and to moor once the necessary reception facilities have been set up and once adequate security personnel – probably the civil police – are on site. This is extremely important as there have been cases where the migrants have jumped vessel as soon as coming alongside the pier. They must not be permitted to avoid questioning by police or immigration personnel.

It is not uncommon for migrants requiring urgent medical attention to be winched off the vessel by rescue helicopter and taken to hospital prior to the vessel's entry into port. It is also unfortunately common to find a number of deceased migrants onboard the vessel on berthing. It is vitally important that the competent authorities are immediately notified of such occurrences as this is invariably followed by a judicial inquiry or similar investigation and certain procedures may need to be followed in order to preserve and collect evidence.

Fortunately, Harbour Masters do not have to deal personally with migrants once they have been taken away from the port facility or harbour area. But this does not mean that the job is finished. Harbour Masters will need to ensure that any records and reports needed are finalised and that any required follow-up action is taken. A debriefing session should be organised with key personnel who participated in the migrant reception operation. This will ensure that any useful comments and suggestions by those involved are considered. Following up the lessons learned will ensure that future operations are conducted much more efficiently and effectively.

The background to this case study is that illegal migration has dramatically increased over the past two decades, especially in the Mediterranean region. Both illegal and general migrants are driven by similar issues: unemployment, poverty, conflicts, war and political persecution.

As border controls have got stricter and many find it impossible to meet visa requirements, more and more people turn to organisations that engage in the trafficking of humans. People risk their lives to cross borders, in addition to spending huge amounts of money. They may be hidden in containers or boats not equipped for transporting human beings and large groups of people are carried across borders and abandoned by smugglers and traffickers if the immigration authorities approach. This makes everyone involved in the venture more desperate.

As it has become more and more expensive for migrants to pay their passage to get into Europe, illegal migrants are searching for other, more economical, ways to make their journeys. Instead of paying someone to ferry them across the Mediterranean, most migrants now pool resources and buy a boat and one of the migrants with a basic knowledge of navigation or sailing is selected to take them all across.

On arrival at the intended destination, the migrants get ashore with the utmost haste and the boat is abandoned. This method will continue to gain popularity as it is cheaper than paying a criminal third party to ferry a migrant party across the Mediterranean. These criminals often throw migrants overboard if law enforcement officials are encountered en-route. The option of taking their own boat is high risk, however, as migrants sail with inexperienced skippers in small boats not built to encounter the rough seas of the Mediterranean.

Countries to the north and the south of the Mediterranean Sea are transit countries as well as destinations. Under EU regulations, especially under the Dublin Convention, Portugal, Spain, France, Italy, Greece, Cyprus and Malta are required to take responsibility for illegal migrants as they enter their territorial seas. As a consequence, illegal migrants see an advantage in not carrying documents as identification could speed repatriation if they are apprehended by law enforcement authorities.

Trafficking entities are often well-organised criminal organisations. As trafficking has become a profitable business, assisting victims of trafficking has become dangerous as well. The criminal organisations regard illegal migrants as their property, and any interference from other individuals attracts retribution.

Refugees and illegal migrants are nothing new in the Mediterranean but attempts to regulate modern migration were addressed with increasing urgency from in the 1990s by States bordering the sea. Now it is abeing tackled by the European Union, with the introduction of Frontex a few years ago. This serves as the EU's maritime policing unit for the Mediterranean, focusing mainly on border control and illegal migration.

Quantifying the scale of the issue is problematic. Records are available for the number of legal migrants, formal asylum seekers, those granted temporary protection status and those formally evacuated from conflict areas. But by definition, illegal migrants are clandestine, seeking to avoid regulation and control by State authorities.

Numbers of those who fail to arrive safely can only be estimated. Interceptions and detentions, which in Spain number approximately 1,500 a year, can only be a rough indicator. According to the EU, estimates of the number of illegal migrants living in Spain, however they arrived, has varied widely but a realistic estimation is about 200,000. The number of refugees reaching Italy and Greece can only be guessed at because large numbers have chosen unregulated or clandestine methods of arrival. According to an EU estimate, about 80,000 to 100,000 refugees and illegal migrants have arrived Italy by boat every 10 years.

If we assume that the number of intercepted seaborne migrants entering Spain can be doubled to account for undetected arrivals, say 3,000 a year since 1996, and a similar number allowed for Greece, then an estimate for the EU countries of the Mediterranean in the decade would probably be in excess of 200,000. Estimating the number of sea voyages also has to take account of the fact that Turkey, Malta, Lampedusa and Cyprus are transit points, and individuals may make more than one voyage in the course of a migration. There is no doubt that in recent years a significant proportion of illegal migrants and refugees reaching the northern Mediterranean States, and probably the majority arriving in Italy, are boat people.

The main routes are:

- From the Maghreb direct to the southern coast of Spain, or via Melilla and Ceuta
- From Turkey to Greece or Sicily
- From the south-eastern Adriatic coast to Italy, and especially Puglia
- From Central, West and East Africa (especially, Somalia, Eritrea, Sudan) via Libya to Malta and Italy
- From Egypt, or the Maghreb via Libya or Tunisia, to Sicily or mainland Italy, sometimes via Malta or Lampedusa

Greece, Italy, and Spain are not necessarily final destinations, of course, and most people then move on to Austria, Germany, Switzerland and the Benelux countries. A trend in the late 1990s and early 2000s, however, was for Italy and Spain to become destinations of residence.

According to UNCLOS, States may exercise jurisdiction over vessels suspected of human smuggling under two circumstances:

- If they infringe their immigration laws
- If they enter the territorial sea en route to a destination within the State

However, a problem arises if the vessel is merely on passage through a State's territorial sea to a third State. In such cases, States may have to look hard at UNCLOS Article 27 to argue that the mere presence of such a vessel in the territorial sea affects the 'peace and good order' of the coastal State. Furthermore, if a vessel involved in trafficking people is not flying a flag or appears to be a vessel without nationality, it may be boarded on the high seas by the warships of any nation.

The International Maritime Organization (IMO) has adopted MSC/Circ.896. Rev.1, an instrument entitled *Interim Measures for the Combating of Unsafe Practices Associated with the Trafficking or Transport of Migrants by Sea*, which is designed to promote awareness and cooperation among contracting Governments. Relevant provisions of this IMO measure are reflected in Chapter II on Smuggling of Migrants by Sea of the Protocol against the Smuggling of Migrants by Land, Air and Sea, supplementing the United Nations Convention against Trans-national Organized Crime.

Actions under these guidelines are primarily the responsibility of flag States. But if it is thought that a foreign vessel is following unsafe practices on the high seas there is provision for requests to be made to its flag State to board, inspect and carry out safety examinations. Then, if evidence is found that the ship is engaged in unsafe practices, the port State may take appropriate action against the vessel, people and cargo onboard, if authorised by the flag State. According to the protocol, such authorisation requests should be granted 'expeditiously'. If a ship is found to be engaged in unsafe practices, the detaining State should report its findings immediately to the flag State and consult on the further actions.

Amendments to the IMO's SOLAS and SAR Conventions concern the treatment of people rescued at sea, or asylum seekers, refugees and stowaways, following a number of incidents.

Captain Rueben Lanfranco BA (Crim) M Jur (Int Law) LL M (IMLI) Dip Mar Sur AMRINA MIFireE MCILT AFRIN FNI FIIMS MIM

Freelance maritime consultant and government authorised ship surveyor, Malta

ABOUT THE AUTHOR

Reuben took up a nautical career following secondary education, serving on merchant vessels and passenger ferries, before joining the Armed Forces of Malta. He then underwent naval officer training at the German Naval Academy and other naval, Coast Guard and Federal Marine Police Institutions in Germany, Italy and the USA. Throughout his career, Rueben has been involved in maritime law enforcement operations and was the founder and the first officer-in-charge of the the Armed Forces of Malta Maritime Rapid Deployment Team. While serving with the armed forces he graduated with a Bachelor's degree in Criminology, and Master's Degrees in International Law and International Maritime Law. Reuben also qualified as a military parachutist and as a certified maritime search and rescue mission coordinator. Following his naval career, he was appointed as the Director of Malta's state-run Maritime College and was responsible for training merchant marine officers.

Reuben is frequently engaged as a flag State and court appointed expert for maritime casualty and incident investigations. He is also a senior trainer for a number of international organisations on maritime affairs and has served as Chairman of The Nautical Institute Malta Branch.

Chapter 16

The Harbour Master and management, finances, training and education

by **Kevin Richardson**, Harbour Master, Dover

Introduction

Today's Harbour Masters are increasingly involved in the day to day management of port operations beyond their technical and statutory roles. In my dealings with Harbour Masters from around the globe, the overwhelming message I hear is one of greater involvement and greater responsibility in the operational and commercial business of a port, beyond the pure maritime elements.

If one accepts this is the general case then the particular skills which form the title of this section are arguably essential for today's Harbour Master, even in the smallest of ports. So what does this mean for the work of the Harbour Master?

Management

There are many quotations which attempt to define management and here are three that I rather like:

Management is all about getting things done through other people
Origin unknown

Good management consists of showing average people how to do the work of superior people
John D. Rockefeller

Managers are people who never put off until tomorrow what they can get other people to do today
Origin unknown

The above statements may be somewhat sweeping generalisations but they really do encapsulate for me what management is all about. Management is indeed about getting things done. That almost inevitably means involving other people in understanding why you want things done, actually getting things done and then checking that things done are delivered according to your requirements. So what are the management skills Harbour Masters need to have in their professional toolboxes? The following list should not contain too many surprises. Indeed any standard management guide or publication would probably come up with a similar list. There are two broad groupings: people management and business management.

- People management competencies
- Communication and influencing

If you are not a skilled communicator you are unlikely to become a competent manager. As a Harbour Master you may be involved with individuals, stakeholders, commercial organisations, government agencies, statutory authorities and a whole range of internal port personnel and external customers. Communicating with such a wide range of interested parties demands knowledge, experience, diplomacy, accuracy, sensitivity and determination to ensure your particular message is conveyed in the most appropriate way. It should also be conveyed in a timely manner and in the language that the intended recipient of the message can readily understand. Does that sound simple? It is in theory, but most Harbour Masters I know have to deal with a myriad of issues on a daily basis at various levels of a port business. These range from a briefing of the board or duty holder, talking to operational staff at the sharp end of operations or discussing business objectives with the Chief Executive.

No-one ever listened themselves out of a job!
Calvin Coolidge US President

Analysis and decision making

The ability to analyse information and data quickly and accurately and to make the right decision in the right timeframe in relation to that analysis is essential. For the Harbour Master this could be relatively simple.

Example

The latest harbour survey reveals shoaling in an area of the approach channel.

Action required: mobilise a dredger to work until correct depths are re-established. A relatively complex subject might involve operational input into a major piece of port infrastructure requiring millions in capital expenditure.

In any moment of decision, the best thing you can do is the right thing; the next best thing you can do is the wrong thing; and the very worst thing you can do is nothing!
Theodore Roosevelt US President

Driving for results

This is all about managing one's own and other's performance. Harbour Masters are senior managers in most ports organisations. Indeed they may also be the Chief Executive in some ports. As such, the way they conduct themselves will come under close scrutiny and will influence their ability to manage the performance of others. Time management, meeting deadlines, effective delegation and monitoring performance objectively are key elements.

Why not go out on a limb … that's where the fruit is!
Will Rodgers, cowboy

Leadership and motivation

Many would put these skills at the very top of the list in terms of importance. A good leader has the ability to inspire people and to motivate them. This can of course, be a force for good or evil. History is littered with leaders who have had a disastrous impact upon those whom they have motivated. There is a balance to be struck.

People ask the difference between a leader and a boss. The leader works in the open and the boss in covert. The leader leads and the boss drives!
Theodore Roosevelt

Managing change

Few would argue that the marine industry, and the port industry in particular, are immune to change. Even in our traditional maritime sector there have been huge advances in technology. Both shipping and ports have been affected by the huge changes in global patterns of trade that have had significant impacts over the past decade. If ports are to remain competitive, or even to survive they have to move with the times in response to global shifts in maritime trade. Harbour Masters must be able to respond to such changes at a local port level and manage those changes efficiently within their sphere of operations. Change is never universally welcomed as it brings uncertainty and may require long-term cultural changes which are the most difficult to deal with. Nevertheless, Harbour Masters must be familiar with the principles and pitfalls of 'change management' within their sphere of operation and influence.

We must become the change we want!
Mahatma Ghandi

Planning and organising

Again, these people skills sound deceptively simple. But get it wrong and chaotic planning and disorganisation result. This applies at all levels in the Harbour Master's sphere of influence from shop floor to board room. Good planning and good organisation should make life easier for Harbour Masters and, equally important, for those who work closely in their sphere of influence. There is another unattributed quotation which sums this up rather well:

If you don't know where you are going, all roads lead there!
Origin unknown

Training and development of oneself and others

The training and development for the Harbour Master position is covered in detail in this book, but it is equally important for others in the Harbour Master's team. Training must be appropriate to the needs of the business. Statutory training must be delivered but development training must not be ignored. Bearing in mind my previous liking for the overall definition of management as: 'all about getting things done through people;' it follows that the more you invest in developing people, the more you are likely to be able to deliver what you want to deliver.

Train for what you need to do, not for what you like to do!
Kevin Richardson

Working with others

For the Harbour Master this is essential. Those that fall into the 'others' category are statutory authorities such as the national maritime and border agencies and regional organisations such as EMSA in Europe and local customers and stakeholders. The others category also includes internal customers and people who are absolutely critical to the maintenance of the services and products you as Harbour Masters are seeking to provide. This is not about being popular with others. It is about being very clear with others about what you expect from them in order to support your work and the overall business objectives as well as providing reciprocal support to others where it is reasonable to do so.

If you are not part of the solution then you must be part of the problem!
Eldridge Cleaver

Business management competencies

Business planning and strategy

As the title would suggest, this skill is aimed at developing business plans and how the port works at both a strategic and a local level. At one end of the management spectrum this skill involves understanding how a port is organised, what its business objectives are and how the teams and people you work with are organised. At the top end of the spectrum it might be about contributing to the development of a long term master plan for the port.

A sly rabbit will have three openings to its den
Chinese Proverb

Commercial planning and marketing

No Harbour Master can operate completely outside a commercial environment. There are certainly some port authorities that deliberately limit their exposure in order to exercise their authority without conflicts of interest or unreasonable commercial pressure. Even if Harbour Masters are not directly involved in commercial aspects of the business they must have at least a basic and, many would argue, a detailed knowledge of the port's commercial activities. This could also include the marketing of the business to existing and potential customers and stakeholders and contributing to maximising revenue and developing markets.

A market is never saturated with a good product but is very quickly saturated with a bad one
Henry Ford

Employment law and practice

This is a global issue. Different port regimes in different countries around the world have differing regulations and approaches. What is common is the need to understand and access those rules and regulations that apply in the Harbour Master's area of operations. It's as much about knowing where to find the right expertise and to be able to access it, as it is about the Harbour Master having any specific expertise.

Even in Britain the trades unions tell me that employment contracts have less protection than in the past
Jacques Delores

Health, safety and the environment

Ports are busy, and by the very nature of their business activities, hazardous places to work. The Harbour Master has a key role to play in keeping everyone safe, be they staff, customers or visitors to the port environment. Harbour Masters must be familiar with relevant health and safety and environmental laws on international, national and local levels.

Harbour Masters must have identified the hazards that are present in a port. They should have risk assessed those hazards and managed those risks down to an acceptable level. This can be described as the ALARP principle – as low as reasonably practicable. Environmental legislation is fast catching up with health and safety in terms of its scope and impact on a port business.

Better a thousand times careful – than once dead!
Proverb

Information and communication technology (ICT)

Harbour Masters cannot, and indeed must not, insulate themselves from technological progress. Nowhere is this more important than being competent in being able to use and apply ICT software to the everyday business of Harbour Masters. There is a huge range of ICT software available on the world market. The trick is to decide what package is most appropriate to you to enable you to manage your operations most effectively and efficiently.

Be nice to nerds … chances are you will end up working for one!
Bill Gates

Project management

Projects come in all shapes and sizes, from multi-million dollar capital projects to small inter-departmental process projects that enable better and more efficient cooperation. If projects impact, or have the potential to impact, on Harbour Masters' activities then it is imperative that they can access those particular projects and if necessary have influence over the outcome. A Harbour Master might actually sponsor a major project such as the building of a new berth or might be requested to provide input and expertise into a particular project in terms of time and resources. Maintenance projects are a particular feature of the Harbour Master's realm when it comes to major assets such as berths and vessels but equally much smaller assets such as lifesaving equipment, pumps, quayside protection and so on. A well maintained port is usually a very clear indicator of a well managed port.

Operations keep the lights on; strategy provides a light at the end of the tunnel; project management is the train engine that moves the organisation forward.
Unattributed

Emergency and contingency planning including business recovery

Even the smallest of marine enterprises can encounter and experience emergencies that can impact directly or indirectly on the port's ability to discharge its business to its customers. When such incidents occur it is imperative that there is a well documented and well drilled emergency response. It must deal with the immediate effects of the incident and, equally importantly, minimise the short, medium and long term impacts on the business. In short, deal with the emergency, minimise its impact on the business and return to normality as soon as possible. By virtue of their role and position in the port's business, Harbour Masters will be deeply involved in emergency planning, contingency arrangements and business recovery.

The Chinese use two brush strokes for a crisis. One brush stroke stands for danger, the other for opportunity. In a crisis be aware of the danger – but recognise the opportunity
J.F. Kennedy

Security management

Many Harbour Masters have been closely engaged in security issues since the advent and application of the ISPS Code. Indeed many Harbour Masters are also port facility security officers (PFSOs) under the ISPS Code. Potentially this can introduce conflicts of interest for Harbour Masters when deciding on the most appropriate response to security incidents or alerts, while trying to maintain business normality. Whether directly involved in the security management regime within a port or not, Harbour Masters must have an intimate knowledge of the ISPS Code and its impact on the port's operations. For more on security and the Harbour Master, see Chapter 9.

Security is the chief enemy of mortals!
William Shakespeare

Financial management:

Behold the fool saith 'put not all thine eggs in one basket' which is but a manner of saying 'scatter your money and attention'; but a wise man saith 'put all your eggs in one basket – and watch that basket'
Mark Twain

The global financial climate could currently be described as sensitive and changeable. There has been a major shift in the primary international growth engines with China and India now leading the way in terms of GDP. Worldwide the ports industry has recently felt the effects of the chill winds of global financial instability and recovery to calmer waters will take time. Most Harbour Masters will have felt the effects of the current (2012) global recession, in one form or other. This will have been either in the form of cancelled or rescheduled capital finance projects or just the general tightening of belts in terms of operational costs. Harbour Masters have had to adjust to the new global financial reality and take a much more proactive approach to financial matters than may have traditionally been necessary.

Financial competence is just another management proficiency which is now increasingly and necessarily part of the Harbour Master's skill set. It is not necessary for Harbour Masters to be economists or indeed accountants. But they must have their fingers on the collective financial pulse of the organisation they work for in order to carry out their role effectively.

The most effective and useful financial information available to Harbour Masters is contained within the management accounts of their organisations. These are an essential component of the financial control system in all but the smallest ports. They enable a port's overall operations to be broken down into a number of specific activities, each of which can be set its own financial objectives and monitored against those objectives. Management accounts provide an early warning of change. In investigating the cause of the change and more importantly, deciding what action is required in response, more detailed information is usually required. Drilling down into the detail of the management accounts usually provides the answers or at least a very good clue to the answers.

The provision of accurate and timely management accounts normally identify clearly between fixed and variable costs against expected revenue in those areas. This facilitates the monitoring of operational budgets throughout the financial year and informs any control decisions that may have to be made.

Generally speaking, the further down an organisation's structure that ownership of the budget process can be driven the better. Staff respond to responsibility when given it. Providing financial information to monitor their own teams and individual budget targets will usually produce results, if delivered accurately and in a timely manner. A real advantage of this process is that staff feel involved and not remote from decisions that may be made for the financial well being of the overall organisation.

In operational budget cost centres, the largest costs are usually associated with people. The more people employed in the delivery of a Harbour Master's role and responsibilities, the larger the operational budget is likely to be and the closer and more detailed the monitoring process has to be. Overtime costs alone can hugely affect overall costs and must be effectively monitored and controlled. Usually costs are monitored and forecasts updated on a monthly basis as a minimum. See cost centre table 16.1 opposite.

The extent of any Harbour Master's financial competence will be a function of their role within the organisation and in general terms, the greater the involvement and responsibility, the greater need for getting down to the numbers.

Training and education

What skills and qualifications does a Harbour Master need in order to carry out the role and how are these skills maintained and progressed over time?

Currently, there is no internationally recognised formal Harbour Master's qualification similar to an STCW certificate of competence. There are still relatively few training packages directed at the role of the Harbour Master. When a port authority or harbour board makes the key appointment of a Harbour Master, the criteria in terms of personal specification and qualifications, is usually the decision of the authority concerned. The decision will be based on what they believe to be an appropriate and acceptable suite of skills and qualifications for their particular port. This may vary greatly; the Harbour Master

16.1 Cost centre table

SEPTEMBER 2011

		Month			YTD				Annual		
Cost Centre	**Name**	**Actual**	**Budget**	**Variance**	**Actual**	**Budget**	**Variance**	**Committed**	**Forecast**	**Budget**	**Variance**
OP001	Operations overheads	21,888	21,961	(73)	192,410	197,589	(5,179)	3,185	263,330	267,326	(3,996)
OP002	Cruise	134,883	161,136	(26,253)	1,002,379	943,287	59,092	172,027	1,101,932	1,062,001	39,931
OP003	Freight clearance facility	74,474	65,143	9,331	700,257	585,758	114,499	762	853,876	795,618	58,258
OP004	Contract cleaning	116,787	113,992	2,795	1,033,381	1,025,924	7,457	334,517	1,383,742	1,367,898	15,844
OP007	Security	169,305	164,555	4,750	1,521,567	1,480,994	40,573	458,299	2,023,319	1,974,659	48,660
OP009	ILO	49,412	49,825	(413)	446,957	445,359	1,598	0	610,796	606,133	4,663
OP010	Cargo	36,432	35,126	1,306	319,082	315,709	3,373	0	431,435	428,404	3,031
OP011	Port control	40,561	44,990	(4,429)	376,406	403,361	(26,955)	0	506,141	548,800	(42,659)
OP012	Pilotage	41,847	36,354	5,493	362,652	326,915	35,737	565	485,039	443,778	41,261
OP013	Tugs and dredger	102,462	101,437	1,025	905,833	912,287	(6,454)	193	1,262,734	1,238,350	24,384
OP014	Marina	51,615	40,935	10,680	400,621	367,992	32,629	73	552,688	499,552	53,136
		839,666	**835,454**	**4,212**	**7,261,545**	**7,005,175**	**256,370**	**969,621**	**9,475,032**	**9,232,519**	**242,513**

of a small leisure-only port may require a different set of skills and qualifications from those required by the Harbour Master of a very large commercial port such as Sydney, Southampton, Rotterdam or Cape Town.

So how do port authorities decide what is the most appropriate skill set and which qualifications support that requirement? Traditionally the answer has been to appoint Harbour Masters who have a marine background and have usually served in a senior capacity at sea. Many Harbour Masters have an STCW Master's certificate of competency and many have served as Master of a ship. Does the Master's certificate satisfy the skill set required of a Harbour Master? Should port authorities automatically judge that the possession of a Master's certificate of competency will automatically deliver a competent Harbour Master?

The answer will depend entirely on the employer's view of the role. If that view is wholly based on marine elements then the possession of a Master's certificate is a pretty good indication of eligibility to apply for the post. But any close inspection of the current STCW Master's syllabus will demonstrate that perhaps there are some areas in port operations that are not comprehensively covered. Moreover, if one accepts the premise stated right at the beginning of this chapter that Harbour Masters are increasingly involved in the general management of ports then the similarity between a pure Master's certificate syllabus to a Harbour Master's job description becomes blurred. In addition to this less than perfect alignment of skills, there is evidence to suggest that the traditional pool of talent for the recruitment of Harbour Masters, such as merchant seafarers holding Master's Certificates, is shrinking.

The industry response worldwide to this conundrum is interesting.

In the UK the UK Harbour Masters Association (UKHMA) is pursuing a Certificate of Competence for Harbour Masters. The certificate will be endorsed by the Maritime and Coastguard Agency and will be a recognised qualification similar to STCW certificates. The curriculum for this UK Certificate is based upon *National Occupational Standards for Harbour Masters*. This was drawn up by the marine industry with Harbour Masters' input and is the responsibility of a national training authority. Assessment against the curriculum will be by an assessment panel which will consider a Harbour Master's qualification by examining physical evidence of compliance against the qualifying criteria. The first UK Harbour Masters Certificates of Competence are expected to be issued in 2012. The assessment process for a Certificate of Competence for Harbour Masters is shown in 16.2 opposite.

In Europe, the tendency is still to employ Harbour Masters who hold Master's Certificates and to build upon this excellent base by adding in the necessary management skills as required. But there are notable exceptions. The Port of Amsterdam, for example, has employed a Harbour Master with no marine qualifications or experience whatsoever. The background of this Harbour Master was a solid business qualification and experience. This approach worked for this particular port but it is still very much the exception rather than the rule.

Worldwide the overwhelming tendency is to recruit from a marine related background

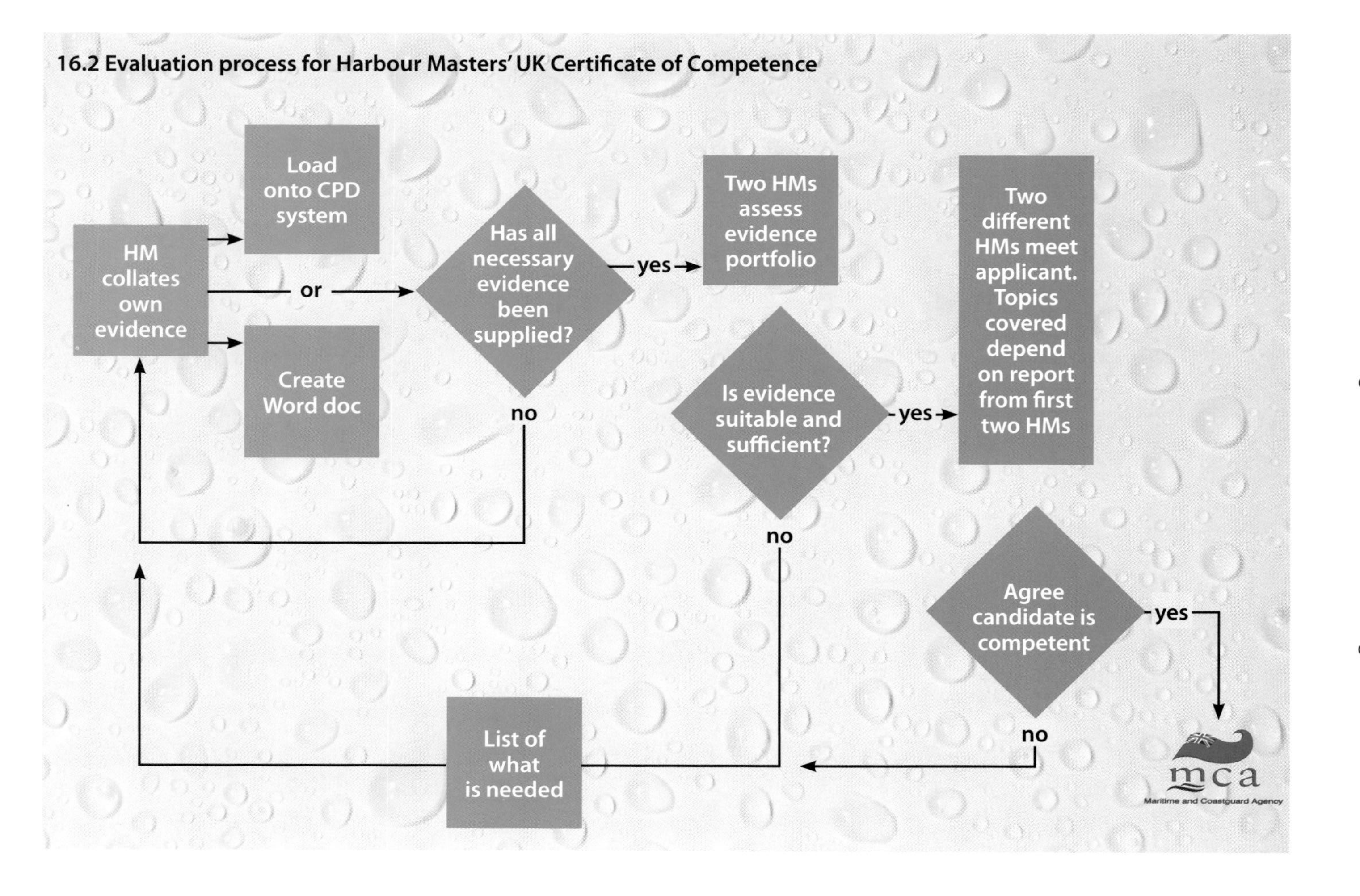

16.2 Evaluation process for Harbour Masters' UK Certificate of Competence

and to require STCW qualifications. This base qualification may then be supplemented by attendance on various courses. These include:

The Harbour Master Certificate Scheme, provided by The Nautical Institute
Diploma in Port Management, provided by IBC Global Academy
Diploma for Harbour Masters, provided by IBC Global Academy
PhD Port Management, provided by World Maritime University

In addition to these specific courses aimed at port management and Harbour Masters there are thousands of courses on general management practice from a myriad of providers worldwide.

There is no move internationally to follow the lead of the UK initiative of a certificate of competency. Much will depend on the uptake and success of the UKHMA initiative. But if it is successful then other organisations in Europe and internationally may well take notice.

In concluding this particular section I will touch upon continuing professional development (CPD) for Harbour Masters. Having been appointed as Harbour Master in particular ports, how do they ensure that they maintain and enhance their level of knowledge, skills and experience and their overall competence? The answer is via a mature continuing professional development programme. Such a system allows a user to identify strengths and weaknesses. It bolsters the strengths and addresses the weaknesses. Professional development can then be planned in a realistic and achievable way and continuously monitored on a rational and verifiable basis.

The UKHMA has had such a system for many years and is now developing and modifying that system to ensure it supports the process of obtaining a Harbour Master's Certificate of Competence. The system should be widely available from 2012. The Nautical Institute also has a continuing professional development programme for its members, serving all sectors of the industry, including Harbour Masters. There may be others around the world but if so, they are not particularly visible.

Conclusion

This chapter has attempted to address the key management, training and educational challenges that are very much part of today's modern Harbour Master. There is very little doubt that the traditional nautical and marine roles are still very important and form a very large part of a Harbour Master's responsibilities. This is only logical as Harbour Masters are fundamentally responsible for the safety of navigation in their ports. But there is little doubt that the role has expanded beyond that purist view and that more and more general management skills are required to discharge these wider responsibilities. In terms of training and education, I have explored a few of the options and initiatives that are underway and available now or in the near future for Harbour Masters. Continuing professional development can, and will, maintain and enhance competence in this vitally important role.

Recommended Reading:

Finance for Non Financial Managers – Roger Mason
Project Management for Dummies – Nick Graham
12 Ladders to World Class Performance – David Drennan, Steuart Pennington

Kevin D Richardson

General Manager Port Operations and Harbour Master Dover

ABOUT THE AUTHOR

Kevin entered service with the merchant navy as a cadet direct from Kingston upon Hull Nautical High School in 1968. He saw 19 years deep-sea service, mainly in reefer and container trades and gained his Masters Foreign Going Certificate in 1984.

He then came ashore and took up a position as VTS operator in the Port of Dover. Transferring from the wet side of operations to the dry side, Kevin moved to terminal operations in 1988 as assistant terminal manager and then to deputy terminal manager in 1990. He was appointed marine services manager in 1997 and head of marine operations/Harbour Master in 2001. He became head of port operations in 2005, general manager in 2008 and Chief Harbour Master in 2012.

From 2008-2012 he served as President of the UK Harbour Masters Association.

As Chief Harbour Master of the busiest ro-ro port in Europe he is responsible to the Board for all compliance issues including the Port marine Safety Code and the ISM Code. He also acts as the port security officer in the newly designated Dover Port Security Authority. Part of his new role is to develop the range of consultancy services this world class port can offer, including port operations, marine operations, master planning, engineering, safety and security.

When he is not in the office Kevin is a fanatical cricket fan and spends not enough time on the golf course in pursuit of a handicap that won't embarrass him!

Chapter 17

The Harbour Master and professional membership

By **Ingrid Römers** and **Bridget Hogan**

At their best, professional membership organisations such as The Nautical Institute and the International Harbour Masters' Association (IHMA) promote professional standards and help career development. Membership of both organisations can only help Harbour Masters understand issues across different disciplines in the maritime industry and enhance their professional standing.

All this may sound theoretical, but there are many practical ways that membership of professional associations will help Harbour Masters. In an industry with little provision for continuing professional development (CPD) they can take advantage of the programmes in place for this. Those promoted by these organisations provide information to help members add to their continuing professional development spanning many areas of the industry. As can be seen by the chapters in this book, the work of Harbour Masters is complex and touches on many areas. It is vital then, that as well as keeping up to date with issues considered directly important to Harbour Masters, they keep in touch with others in the industry – not least potential users of their facilities.

The Nautical Institute, set up in 1972, was from the first concerned to see excellence in areas not necessarily covered in certificate examinations, including general areas such as leadership and more specific sectors such as the work of Harbour Masters. To help promote the understanding of these nautical disciplines, the Institute became a publisher of industry standards – including those established in *The Work of the Harbour Master*, of which this book is the third edition.

The Institute has promoted cooperation at a professional level worldwide between all disciplines of the nautical sciences, helping to enhance better mutual understanding of design and operational issues. It holds a series of Command Seminars around the world every three years to examine professional issues and reports on the proceedings. There is a network of over 40 branches in the major maritime nations of the world which hold events where members have an opportunity to pass on their own skills and learn from the experiences of other.

All this work is bound together by a five-year Strategic Plan. It addresses industry-wide issues that Institute members decide, through a consultation, that they want to see addressed. This can include areas such as piracy and maritime security; competency, manning levels; recruitment and retention; evolving technologies; criminalisation and fair treatment of seafarers, together with professional development.

Together the aim is to improve the professionalism of members and the Institute's work with the IHMA shows how this professional ethos can be spread throughout the industry. The IHMA was founded in 1994. In the years leading up to its formation, European Harbour Masters had worked together in what is called the European Harbour Masters' Committee (EHMC), reaching out internationally to expand and to gain IMO consultative status.

The IHMA has grown and now has membership from most major maritime regions. It also works to promote professionalism and has several ways of achieving this. Every two years it holds an international congress to spread new ideas and professionalism; most members in the association know each other personally and the association offers a service in which members can seek the advice of fellow members.

From 2010, the IHMA looked at new ways of benefitting members and has drawn up a strategy to this end. First the position of IHMA Development Officer (IDO) was established, with the first appointment going to Jaap Lems, former EHMC Chairman, Vice-President of the IHMA, Chief Harbour Master of the Port of Rotterdam and a contributor to this book. His task was to draw up proposals to enable the association to enhance its professional standing, make it more relevant to Harbour Masters and the general maritime community and to encourage more member involvement.

Compared to other organisations in the field, the IHMA is small in terms of budget, membership, organisation and structure as would be expected from a young association; but it is building a solid foundation for growth. Other associations have offered advice; a board member of the International Association of Ports & Harbors said: "Make sure that there is continuity, show that you exist and make sure you stay!"

Expanding the profile

IHMA membership and association work needs to reflect the added value nautical professionals contribute to their ports in two areas: operationally and financially. The IHMA should stand out as a group of select individuals with collective specialist knowledge in the unique services provided by its members. They offer added value to the ports they serve.

The association is based on individual membership in a profession limited to a small group of people – probably not more than 3,000 worldwide.

Organising the work

There is now a strategic plan to develop IHMA as a relevant association with professional standing and a positive image under the IDO and Mr Lems. The IHMA will expand its influence and build membership.

Members who help IHMA in this task will benefit from being involved in these improvement projects, gaining information and adding to their personal networks. The IHMA is a volunteer organisation, and this can mean participants having to balance work for the association and for their port. As was shown in the tremendous response to this book, a joint project between IHMA and The Nautical Institute, members can be very generous of their time and knowledge for the good of all Harbour Masters.

The IHMA has shown, with projects such as these that it can act as an umbrella organisation and can reach out to other organisations to share information and expertise from all over the world, either on a regional or worldwide basis.

There is great potential for the IHMA and for Harbour Masters to improve their own professionalism and their profile. There is a great deal of commitment to the industry and goodwill towards the association. Most Harbour Masters believe that in future there will be an increased need for a specialist professional membership organisation like the IHMA as well as a more general one like The Nautical Institute and we can see a bright future ahead of us!

Bridget Hogan
Director
Publishing and Marketing
The Nautical Institute

ABOUT THE AUTHOR

Bridget joined The Nautical Institute in 2008 after a career in the maritime and publishing industries. She has worked in senior management for shipowning and ship management companies with fleets which included tankers, general cargo and reefer vessels. She also has held senior posts for a flag state, a stock exchange, The Baltic Exchange, Lloyd's Register and the Renault group. Her publishing career has included time at *Lloyd's List*, *Fairplay* and other maritime publications. She has edited a local newspaper and has been involved in training and mentoring in publishing over the years. Outside of the office she is interested in sports such as running, cycling, swimming and canoeing, countryside crafts and conservation and serves as a school governor.